CHICAGO TO THE SEA

LECTOR HOUSE PUBLIC DOMAIN WORKS

HAPPY READING!

CHICAGO TO THE SEA

WILLIAM C. GAGE

ISBN: 978-93-5420-923-9

Published: 1883

© 2021
LECTOR HOUSE LLP

LECTOR HOUSE LLP
E-MAIL: lectorpublishing@gmail.com

CHICAGO TO THE SEA

EASTERN EXCURSIONIST

A COMPLETE GUIDE
TO THE
PRINCIPAL ✢ EASTERN ✢ SUMMER ✢ RESORTS.
INCLUDING NIAGARA FALLS, THE WHITE MOUNTAINS,
SAINT LAWRENCE AND SAGUENAY RIVERS,
MONTREAL AND QUEBEC,
THE NEW ENGLAND SEA BEACHES, ETC.,
AND HOW AND WHEN TO ENJOY THEM.

BY

WILLIAM C. GAGE,

AUTHOR OF "THE SWITZERLAND OF AMERICA,"
"HAND-BOOK OF TRAVEL,"
"PLEASURE RESORTS OF THE GREAT NORTHWEST,"
"GOOD BEHAVIOR AT HOME AND ABROAD," ETC.

1883.

CONTENTS

CONTENTS

vii

NOTES—INTRODUCTORY.

I.—EASTWARD HO!

hile it is true that the great tide of travel, like the "star of empire," is ever westward, and the iron-bound highways leading toward the setting sun are the channels through which this current surges with ever-increasing volume, yet like those of the ocean, this tide has its ebb as well as flow. The business relations which exist between the East and the West render necessary a constant inter-communication, which of itself is sufficient to account for much of the returning travel. In addition to this, the social relations also exert their influence. The man who "went West" to make his fortune desires to revisit the home of his youth on the Eastern hillside. Perhaps his children, who have grown up on the prairies, wish to see the hills and valleys so often described by their parents, and contrast the almost boundless expanses of the "great West" with the rugged mountain scenery and the rocky farms, where unceasing toil, coupled, perhaps, with honest poverty, laid the foundation for sterling integrity, which the ease and freedom of Western life have not served to obliterate.

The attractions of the natural scenery of the East are of themselves sufficient to call to them annually thousands of tourists, who, independently of the causes already mentioned, occupy their "summer vacations" with an Eastern tour simply for the enjoyment of the attractions presented in the way of pleasant routes of travel, and the scenery to be enjoyed on the way or at the objective point of the journey.

With a view of meeting the wants of this great and constantly increasing class of excursionists, this work has been written. It is designed to point out the most desirable routes between Chicago and the Eastern seaboard, and to serve as a book of ready reference by the way. The lines of travel chosen are such as will give the tourist the most favorable opportunities for visiting the celebrated summer resorts *en route*, and secure the advantages of palace coaches, dining cars, quick transit, and sure connections,—considerations which combine to make a journey enjoyable, and by means of which a trip becomes a luxury as a means as well as an end.

The descriptions are made simple and practical, and with no effort to impart a roseate hue to the scenes described, but with a view to aid the tourist in "seeing with his own eyes" the beauties of landscape or other scenery from the most favorable points of observation, and discover for himself the things too often seen only through the medium of the guide book.

II.—SUMMER TRAVEL.

The benefits arising from a summer jaunt, with its release from the cares of business, are of inestimable value. "Work and worry" are killing hundreds who might be saved to long life and happiness could they but break away from their toil for a trip to the mountains or seaside, or some other place where business could for the time be forgotten. Though the respite be only a brief one, a break in the monotony of a busy life will sometimes relieve the tension which if too long continued snaps asunder the strings which need relaxation to preserve their strength.

The man who esteems his life work too important to admit of vacations sometimes learns, when too late for remedy, that unremitting application to his task has totally disqualified him for its continuance, and long before the period when he ought to be in his prime, he is compelled to relinquish to others the work he so fondly hoped to finish himself. A little relaxation now and then might have saved him from a collapse, but "he couldn't afford the time."

Happily for the American business world, the infection of "summer travel" grows more and more contagious as its benefits become better understood. Year by year the tide increases in volume, and the facilities of travel are multiplied to meet the demand. If these pages shall serve to assist the tourist in the choice of his route, or, the choice being made, in rendering his journey more enjoyable, their purpose will be fully met.

CHICAGO TO THE SEA.

THE STARTING POINT.

hicago, the great metropolis of the Northwest, with its multitude of railroad lines, and its enormous commercial interests, is most naturally the point of departure for east-bound tourists. Travelers from localities west of Chicago will desire to tarry in the city for a brief period, to visit its water-works, the grand exposition building, and the variety of other objects of interest which render the place attractive to strangers. In carrying out this purpose, they will find the hotel accommodations of the city to be second to none in America. The Grand Pacific, Palmer, Clifton, Briggs, Sherman, Merchants, and a host of others of good repute, invite the tourist to share their hospitalities, with the assurance of regal fare and sumptuous accommodations. For full information in regard to Chicago hotels and their terms, the reader is referred to the *Daily National Hotel Reporter*, which gives reliable and complete advices on this subject.

The limits of this work forbid even a mention of the many objects of interest to be seen in Chicago; and having to do with the city only as the starting point for our tourist, we next settle the question as to the route by which our Eastern journey is to be performed. Keeping in view the important points of speed, safety and comfort, together with the attractiveness of the scenery *en route*, we find the claims of

THE MICHIGAN CENTRAL RAILROAD

To be of a character to meet all the requirements of the most exacting traveler. It has long been known as the NIAGARA FALLS ROUTE, and its recent acquirement of the Canada Southern Railway, making now a continuous line from Chicago to the very verge of the famous cataract, more fully than ever entitles it to that appellation. Its through sleeping-car connections, its superior equipment, its famous dining-cars, together with the attractive country which it traverses, and the many interesting points reached by it, all combine to decide the question of superiority, and influence the tourist in his choice of routes.

The traveler arriving in Chicago by other roads, and not desiring to tarry in the city, can be immediately transferred by Parmelee's omnibus line to the depot of the Michigan Central, at the foot of Lake street, and taking his seat in a Wagner drawing-room car, commence his journey with baggage checked through to destination, and with the assurance that his comfort will be carefully considered on the part of the train employés from the beginning of his trip to the end of the road.

THE CELEBRATED FAST EXPRESS

Of this road leaves Chicago in the afternoon, and as all first-class tickets are accepted on this train without extra charge, it is a favorite with the traveling public. In the season of summer travel, it is a popular tourists' train, on account of its timely arrival at Niagara, allowing the excursionist to spend the entire day at the Falls, and take the evening train for the St. Lawrence River, which is reached at Clayton the next morning. From this point, the elegant day boats of the St. Lawrence Steamboat Company make the trip down the river to Montreal, *via* Round Island Park, the celebrated Thousand Islands, the famous Rapids, and past the most lovely scenery of this beautiful river, which stoutly contests with the Hudson the claim to the title of the "Rhine of America." The entire journey is by daylight, the boats reaching Montreal at 6 P. M. This trip, which will be more fully described in its proper place, constitutes one of the delightful features of the excursion "to the sea," and has been immensely popularized by the efforts of the St. Lawrence Steamboat Company, which is the only line down the St. Lawrence running boats exclusively for passenger service. It has won its way to the favor of the traveling public in the two past years of successful operation, being popularly known as the New American Line.

But to return to the point of digression. Leaving Chicago by any of the express trains of the Michigan Central, the tourist has at his service all the facilities which make pleasant a journey by rail. The celebrated Wagner drawing-room and sleeping cars are run through to New York and Boston without change, dining cars are attached to the trains at convenient hours for meals, and courteous and attentive conductors, train men, porters, etc., contribute to the comfort and pleasure of the traveler as occasion presents for their services.

The ride out of the city and through the suburbs for a considerable distance is along the shores of Lake Michigan, presenting views of the lake craft, with their white sails, or clouds of smoke and vapor from their stacks, as far as the eye can reach. The government pier, with its protecting wall, stretches along the shore, and in the distance may be seen the "crib" of the water-works.

On the other hand, the Douglas monument and park present themselves to view, together with numerous interesting objects peculiar to the suburbs of a great city, until, increasing its speed, the train passes fairly into the open country, which is here and there dotted with a suburban residence, or the buildings of some thrifty farmer, or perchance a pretty village, whose inhabitants have their business interests in Chicago, but their homes in the quiet suburbs of the bustling city.

Fifteen miles out, we pass the charming town of PULLMAN, a model settlement, sometimes called the "magic city," with its elegant buildings, all of brick, in the most approved styles of architecture. Its important industrial enterprises are largely connected with the interests of travel, comprising the Allen paper car-wheel shops, the Pullman car manufactory, and various other establishments which contribute to the prosperity of this flourishing town.

At about this stage of the journey, if on board the Fast Express, or the later train known as the Atlantic, the tourist is greeted with the welcome announcement, from a man in white cap and apron, looking as though he had just stepped in from the Palmer House café,

"DINNER NOW READY IN THE DINING CAR."

Among the modern comforts of railway traveling, the dining-car system takes a prominent place. The hasty scramble for refreshments at a wayside restaurant, with the constant fear of "getting left," and a consequent bolting of half-masticated food, with dyspepsia in its train, now gives place to a leisurely eaten meal, served in elegant style, with all the appointments and conveniences that can be suggested by the most refined taste. The Michigan Central was among the first to adopt this innovation, and so popular has it become as an adjunct to their already long list of popular features, that they have recently constructed four of these elegant hotels upon wheels, and placed them upon their line between Chicago and Niagara Falls. These dining cars are models of taste, elegance and convenience, with spacious kitchens, store rooms and lavatories, large plate-glass windows, folding or opera chairs, and in fact every convenience that taste and experience could suggest for the comfort of their patrons.

A glance at the *menu*, which is as complete as that of a first-class hotel attests the fact that the gratification of its patrons, and not profit to its treasury, is the first great aim of the company in operating the dining-car system. Indeed, it may well be questioned how such elegant meals can be furnished for the sum of seventy-five cents, when a similar repast at many a hotel in the land would cost from one to two dollars. Perhaps a solution of the problem may be found in the remark of a shrewd Yankee, who once sat opposite the writer at table in one of these cars. He had evidently fasted for many hours previous, as his voracious appetite clearly indicated. On rising from the table, he soliloquized thus: "Well, I guess this concern han't made much out o' me this time, but I shall *allus come by this route hereafter*."

The dining-car system is also in successful operation on the Canada division of the Michigan Central, the equipments and appointments being of the same character and completeness. Indeed, so popular has this feature become, that several other cars are in course of construction to extend the system in a manner to meet every demand of the public for accommodation in this direction.

But while we have been thus indulging in reflections on this subject, the train has been speeding onward, and here we are at MICHIGAN CITY, on the extreme southern shore of Lake Michigan, and the great lumber port of Northern Indiana. It is a railroad center of some importance, the Indianapolis, Peru & Chicago, and Louisville, New Albany & Chicago Railroads occupying the union depot with the Michigan Central. The population is about eight thousand, and its principal business interests are manufacturing and lumber. The view of the city from the car windows gives a less favorable impression of the place than a closer inspection entitles it to, the immense sand bluffs and unpretending buildings on the lake shore being the most conspicuous objects near the track. The city proper is quite an attractive and pleasant locality. Its chief hotels are the St. Nicholas, Union and Jewell.

Ten miles further eastward, we reach NEW BUFFALO, the southern terminus of the Chicago & West Michigan Railroad, which from this point skirts the eastern shore of Lake Michigan, forming the shore line to Pentwater. It is a pretty little town of about one thousand inhabitants.

Passing several stations at which the express trains make no stop, twenty miles further on we reach NILES, a flourishing city of nearly five thousand inhabitants.

The Michigan Central has a branch road running from this point to South Bend, and it is also the western terminus of its "Air Line" division, the other being Jackson. Much of the freight business of the road is done over this division, relieving the main line for the better accommodation of its immense passenger traffic. Mercantile and manufacturing interests occupy the attention of the thriving people of Niles, a superior water power furnishing excellent facilities for flour and paper mills and other enterprises, which combine to make this an important business center. Its leading hotels are the Bond, Pike and Farler.

At LAWTON, thirty-one miles from Niles, connection is made with the Paw Paw Railroad for Hartford, Lawrence and Paw Paw. The express trains do not stop, however, but, hurrying onward, the next important station is that so well known as the "Big Village."

Kalamazoo, with a population of about twelve thousand, and no city charter, prides itself on being one of the largest villages in America. Except in its municipality, however, it is, to all intents and purposes, a city, with its extensive public works, its thriving manufacturing establishments, and its important railroad interests. The South Haven division of the Michigan Central extends westward from here to the shore of Lake Michigan. Intersection is also made with the Grand Rapids & Indiana Railroad and the Kalamazoo division of the Lake Shore Railway. The manufacturing and mercantile interests of Kalamazoo are quite extensive, and it has also acquired no little celebrity as a market for superior agricultural products. Its leading hotels are the Burdick House, Kalamazoo House and American House.

Battle Creek, twenty-three miles east of Kalamazoo, is the next important city on the route, and is one of the most thriving and enterprising towns in the State. Many of its business interests are on an extensive scale, notably the manufacture of threshing machinery and engines, three large establishments being devoted to this industry. On approaching the city the buildings of the *Review & Herald* Publishing establishment are among the first to attract attention, and just before the train comes to a halt, it passes the shops of the Battle Creek Machinery Company, which are on the left of the track, while the factory of the Union School Furniture Company is nearly opposite, on the right. The products of the former company are shipped to all parts of the world, while the "Automatic" school-seat is acquiring a national reputation as one of the most convenient and unique articles of furniture ever put in use in a school-room.

The intersection of the Michigan Central, the Chicago & Grand Trunk, and the Toledo & Milwaukee Railroads, the latter just completed, renders Battle Creek an important railroad center, and accounts for the rapid and prosperous growth of the city. This is also the location of the

CELEBRATED MEDICAL AND SURGICAL SANITARIUM,

Which has gained an enviable reputation as an invalid's home. Although not originally designed as a summer resort, its facilities in that direction have made it a favorite summer home for many who would hardly call themselves invalids. Here may be found a remedy for one great drawback to the success of summer vacations in general, which are often robbed of much of their sanitary benefit by poor food and inattention to the laws of health. While the *cuisine* of this establishment is of the most bounteous character, it is especially ordered with reference to healthfulness, and is in itself one important element of the great success of the institution in curing the sick.

The facilities of the Sanitarium for the treatment of disease are the best known to modern medical science. In addition to baths of every description, including Turkish, Russian, vapor, electro-vapor, thermal, etc., the employment of massage, Swedish movements, and the various forms of electrical treatment, are provided for by costly appliances, some of which were designed expressly for this institution. When we add that the medical superintendent, Dr. J. H. Kellogg, is a member of the State Board of Health, and occupies a position of great prominence as a writer and lecturer on sanitary matters, and that a staff of educated and intelligent gentlemen and lady physicians are constantly caring for patients and visitors, we have indicated some of the reasons for the marvelous prosperity of the institution. Our illustration gives a view of the main building. A large number of cottages and other buildings make up the facilities of the SANITARIUM for taking care of its guests.

MEDICAL AND SURGICAL SANITARIUM.—MAIN BUILDING.

The leading hotels of Battle Creek are the Lewis House and the Williams House, the Sanitarium being also a favorite transient home with many travelers.

Shortly after leaving the station at Battle Creek, the train comes to a halt at the crossing of the Chicago & Grand Trunk Railway, at the station named Nichols, the location of the extensive works where are manufactured the celebrated Nichols, Shepard & Co.'s "Vibrator" threshing machinery, engines, etc. This is one of the most important industries of the city, giving employment to a large number of skilled mechanics. Just beyond are the railroad shops of the C. & G. T. Company, which also furnish employment to a goodly number of men.

MARSHALL, the next important station, is a pleasant little town, the county seat of Calhoun county, with some manufacturing interests, and considerable wealth, being the center of a large and prosperous agricultural district. It is widely known among travelers as the dining station of the Michigan Central Railroad. The day trains still make their stops here for dinner, and the hours of midday are among the liveliest the people of this quiet place witness. It is the boast of the managers of the dining-rooms that a failure to provide chicken pie for their guests has occurred but once in seventeen years, although fabulous prices often have to be paid for the feathered bipeds to perpetuate the time-honored custom.

The Tontine, Forbes and Tremont Houses are the principal hotels.

ALBION is the next town of much importance in our journey, and is really a thriving place, some of its manufactures being widely known. It is also the seat of Albion College, a flourishing denominational school, under the management of the Methodists. Our road here intersects the Lansing division of the Lake Shore Railway. The principal hotels of Albion are the Commercial and the Albion House.

Our next important station is JACKSON, the largest city in the interior of the State. As the central point of heavy railroad interests, important manufactures, and extensive commercial enterprises, the city is well known. The State prison is located here, and is of itself a manufacturing establishment of no little importance. The railroad shops of the Michigan Central give employment to nearly a thousand men, and thus contribute largely to the city's prosperity. The mineral resources of the vicinity are of no small magnitude, comprising coal, salt, fire clay, etc.

It is the terminus of the Grand River Valley, Air Line, and Saginaw divisions of the Michigan Central Railroad and the Fort Wayne and Jackson branches of the Lake Shore and Michigan Southern Railway. Passengers change here for the pleasure resorts of northern Michigan, *via* the Mackinaw Division of the Central, with which connection is made at Bay City.

The Hibbard House, the Hurd House, the Commercial, and several smaller hotels, take good care of travelers who have occasion to tarry in Jackson.

Thirty-eight miles west of Detroit, the train halts at ANN ARBOR, the county seat of Washtenaw county, which has a resident population of about ten thousand, not including the students of the State University, which number nearly fifteen hundred. The city is pleasantly situated on both sides of the Huron River, its streets being wide, finely laid out, and adorned with shade trees. The Toledo,

Ann Arbor & Grand Trunk Railway gives the place a north and south business outlet, while the Central takes care of the east and west business. The Huron River furnishes excellent water power, and the flourishing industries of the city show how well it is improved.

UNIVERSITY OF MICHIGAN.

In addition to all these, its reputation as an educational center places it among the most important of Michigan cities. Its local public schools are of a high order of excellence, especially its High School, which occupies an elegant building costing $50,000. But its chief importance in this respect is from the fact of its being the seat of the University of Michigan, with its departments of literature, science and arts, law, medicine, pharmacy, dental surgery, and engineering. This institution has almost a world-wide reputation as one of the foremost schools in the land, and indeed many of its students are from abroad, attracted by its fame, and the excellent facilities at their command.

The St. James, Cook, and Leonard Houses, are the principal hotels.

YPSILANTI, eight miles distant from Ann Arbor, is the next stopping place, and is a pleasant town of some five thousand inhabitants. The fine water power of Huron River is here utilized by several manufactories, among which that of paper-making is brought to a high state of excellence. In addition to the railroad facilities afforded by the Michigan Central, it has southerly communication by means of a branch of the Lake Shore & Michigan Southern Railway. It is the seat of the State Normal School, which occupies an elegant building, and beautiful grounds, the latter donated to the State for the purpose. There are many fine residences here, some of them the homes of business men of Detroit.

STATE NORMAL SCHOOL.

The Roberts, Lewis, and Hawkins Houses, the European, and several others, furnish adequate hotel accommodations.

From Ypsilanti, the train speeds swiftly over the smoothest of tracks, past pleasant villages, through verdant fields, and in view of snug farm-houses, the next important stopping places being WAYNE JUNCTION, where connection is made with the Flint & Pere Marquette Railroad, and SPRINGWELLS, formerly Grand Trunk Junction, three miles beyond which is

DETROIT, THE CITY OF THE STRAIT.

The largest city in Michigan, and its commercial metropolis, it is beautifully situated on the Detroit River, 18 miles from Lake Erie, and 7 from Lake St. Clair. It is one of the prettiest, pleasantest cities in all the West, and the oldest, as well. Its rapid growth during the past twenty years is a marked feature in connection with its history. The many lines of railroad centering here, and its extensive commercial interests, together with the rich agricultural region which here finds an outlet for its products, all contribute to the prosperity of the city.

The excursionist will find much to interest in a visit to Detroit. Its location upon the river, which is here about half a mile wide, suggests excursions by water, which constitute a considerable share of the recreation of its people, by the numerous lines of steamers which ply between the city and various points on the river and the lakes. The public parks of the city afford pleasant "breathing places" for those who choose to avail themselves of their advantages. In addition to the older resorts of this class, the city has recently purchased Belle Isle, with an area of about 800 acres, and a park commission are engaged in the work of improvement, the result of which will be the providing of a place of recreation for citizens and visitors, comparing favorably with the parks of any of the large cities. Boats leave at frequent intervals for the Island, from the foot of Woodward Avenue.

To notice the many attractions which tempt the tourist to prolong his stay in the beautiful City of the Strait would require too much of our space. We can only add that the resources of the vicinity in the way of entertainment and recreation are ample, and of sufficient variety to render a visit to the city an occasion of much enjoyment. The hotel facilities are unexcelled, comprising fifty or more, including the Antisdel, Brunswick, Griswold, Madison, Michigan Exchange, Rice's Temperance, St. Charles, Russell, and a variety of lesser houses, at all prices. At those above mentioned, the terms range from $1 to $3.50 per day.

CROSSING THE FERRY.

Continuing our eastward journey from Detroit, the river is crossed to the Canada shore by means of the ferry, and the transhipment of the train is an operation of much interest to one who observes it for the first time. The mammoth transfer boat, capable of holding, in several sections, the long passenger train, is securely fastened to the dock, and the cars are run on, with their load of passengers and baggage. The powerful machinery of the boat is set in motion, and in a few moments the train is again made up at Windsor, on the Canada side, ready to proceed on its way.

Windsor, the western terminus of the Canada division of the Michigan Central Railroad, is a flourishing town of about eight thousand inhabitants directly across the river from Detroit. The town of Sandwich, two miles below, has some celebrity as a summer resort on account of its mineral springs.

The chief interest of the American tourist in regard to Canada, however, is in getting through it. While there are many things worthy of note in connection with the homes of our cousins over the border, they are best appreciated by a longer tarry than can be afforded by the excursionist who makes a flying trip between the West and the East. The prejudice of the native American, so frequently manifested against everything Canadian, is often as unfounded as it is unreasonable. To be sure, the difference between Canada and the States in habits and customs is sometimes quite marked, but frequently not more so than that existing between different sections of our own country. The railroad is doing much toward the annihilation of all these differences, by facilitating intercourse and the comingling of the people of all sections.

The trip through Canada is *via* the Canada division, formerly the

CANADA SOUTHERN RAILWAY,

And is the only line through Canada under distinctively American management. While the Michigan division of the road contributes a large amount of local business, even to the express trains, the less populous districts of Canada are sufficiently accommodated by the local trains, allowing the through expresses to make long and rapid runs, with few stops. The fast New York express, for instance, is timed to make the run from Windsor to St. Thomas, a distance of 111 miles, with only a single stop, about midway. The level country through which the road passes, with the long stretches of air line, many miles in extent, are conducive to smooth and rapid running, and in this respect amply compensates for any lack of beauty in the natural scenery. There are, however, some quite interesting sections of country on the route.

St. Thomas, about midway of the line, is a city of some eight or nine thousand inhabitants, and of considerable importance as a railroad center. We here cross the Great Western division of the Grand Trunk, and connect with the St. Clair division of the Michigan Central, and the Credit Valley Railway for Toronto. The leading hotels are the Commercial, Queens, Hutchinson, Wilcox and Lisgar.

At Niagara Junction the train divides, and that portion having Buffalo for its objective point, proceeds, by way of Fort Erie and Black Rock, to the Union Depot in Buffalo, while the other portion goes to America's greatest pleasure resort *via* the Niagara Falls division of the road.

Should the tourist choose to first visit Buffalo, he may proceed to the Falls by later trains, which run at frequent intervals during the day between the two points.

THE CITY OF BUFFALO

Is of interest to the excursionist as one of the most important commercial centers west of New York City, and the focus of a large number of railroads. It has a magnificent harbor, one of the best on the whole chain of lakes, its water front extending about five miles, half on Lake Erie and half on Niagara River. Its grain elevators, some thirty in all, have a storage capacity of nearly six millions of bushels, and are capable of transferring about half that amount every twenty-four hours. As the western terminus of the Erie Canal, and with its lake shipping and railroad facilities, it has become the largest grain port in America, with the single exception of New York City.

The traveler who may wish to prolong his stay in Buffalo will find a multitude of hotels, of all degrees of excellence.

NIAGARA FALLS.

O f all the pleasure resorts on the American continent, probably none receive annually so many visitors as the famous cataract where the waters of the upper lakes so grandly plunge over the precipice on their way to Lake Ontario. The reasons for this are, doubtless, first, the wonderful attractiveness of the Falls as an object of interest, and, secondly, their ease of access, and the consequent facility with which they may be visited. Situated upon the main thoroughfare between the East and the West, over which such a constant tide of travel is surging throughout the entire year, it requires but little sacrifice of time on the part of many to pay them a visit. But these are merely the casual visitors, in addition to whom thousands annually come from all parts of the land, and from over the ocean, to gaze upon this far-famed cataract.

We design to give in this chapter such facts as shall serve as a complete guide for the tourist in visiting this resort, not only to all the points of interest, but such other information as shall render his visit enjoyable. Before entering into particulars, we present a general description of Niagara, in a comprehensive view, which will assist the reader in understanding the several detailed descriptions which follow.

Niagara River is the outlet of Lake Erie, connecting it with Ontario, the lowest in the great chain of lakes, which unitedly are the largest inland reservoirs in the world. The river is only 33 miles in length, and the total descent in that distance is 334 feet, Lake Ontario being that much lower than Erie, which is 565 feet above sea level. About a mile above the Falls the waters commence to descend with great velocity, constituting what is known as the Rapids, second in interest only to the Falls themselves, and adding to the interest of the latter by giving such an increased velocity to the water in its plunge over the precipice. The total descent in this mile is 52 feet, and the waters come rushing and tumbling along the rocky bed of the stream, which is here considerably narrower than its general channel above.

Just above the Falls are several small islands, connected by a system of bridges with one another and the American shore, and affording a magnificent view of the Rapids. Standing on one of the bridges, or the upper shore of an island, and looking up the stream, the view presented is grand and impressive, as the resistless torrent seems ready to overwhelm all in its course.

These islands, combined with a sharp curve in the course of the stream, widen the channel to about 4,750 feet, one-fourth of which is occupied by Goat Island, the largest of the group, which here extends to the extreme verge of the precipice, and divides the stream and the Falls into two distinct parts.

The American Fall is about 1,100 feet wide, and the remainder, or Canada fall, about double the width, although from its curved or horseshoe shape the line of the brink is considerably longer than the direct breadth.

Our illustration presents a fine view of the American Fall from below, looking northward. The waters here make a sheer descent of 164 feet, while the height of the Canadian Fall is from 12 to 14 feet less, owing to the lengthening of the Rapids and the curve of the stream.

The volume of water in the Canada Fall is much greater, however, than that of the American, and the impetus given by the Rapids carries the water over the precipice with great velocity, and it forms a grand curve in the descent, falling clear of the rocky wall into the bed of the river below. The lower strata of this wall being of a loose, shaly character, the action of the spray has hollowed it out, so that between the wall of rock and the descending wall of water, a cavernous space exists, into which the tourist may venture by a rocky and somewhat perilous path from the Canada side. It is needless to add that a water-proof suit adds materially to the comfort of those who thus venture. Similar trips may be made under the American Fall, which will be duly described in detail.

Below the Falls, on the American side, is a stairway and an inclined-plane railway, leading to the water's edge, and connecting with a ferry which here crosses to the Canada shore by means of small boats, amid the spray and over the turbulent waters, not yet at rest from their mighty plunge.

The banks below the Falls are very high and precipitous, and the channel contracts to less than a thousand feet, varying in the descent to Lake Ontario, from 200 to 400 yards.

The entire river, from its source to its mouth, is an interesting geological study. The changes that have taken place in the formation of its banks, and the topography of the country through which it passes, furnish much food for conjecture, upon which several theories have been constructed, one of which seems to be quite universally adopted, viz., that the Falls have gradually receded from a point below their present location, some say as far down as the high bluff at Lewiston, seven miles from Lake Ontario.

This recession is due to the action of the water upon the sections of the rocky bed which have successively formed the verge of the cataract, and which have doubtless varied in character along the course of the river. The action of the spray and the violence of the rebounding waters, combined perhaps with other causes, wore away the softer, shaly substratum, until the harder but thinner upper stratum could no longer support the massive weight and resist the velocity of the waters, and fell into the channel below. This theory is abundantly supported not only by the appearance of the Falls and the channel, but by several occurrences of exactly this character. In 1818, massive fragments fell from the American fall, and in 1828 a like occurrence took place in the Horseshoe Fall, in each instance producing a concussion like an earthquake.

AMERICAN FALL, FROM BELOW.

A view of the Falls by Father Hennepin, made in the year 1678, presents the feature of a distinct fall on the Canada side, somewhat like that on the American side, or nearly at right angles with the main fall. This was occasioned by a great rock, which divided the current and turned a portion of it in that direction, and which has evidently since fallen. (See engraving on page 29.)

How long a time would be required for the Falls to recede to Lake Erie, is of course conjectural, as no data of sufficient reliability can be established from which to make a calculation. Indeed, it is believed by some geologists that higher up the river the formation of the bed is of such a character as to successfully resist the further encroachments of the water in that direction, the hard formation being of greater depth and firmness.

But to the present generation Niagara Falls will remain an object of great interest, and will doubtless continue to receive, as in the past, the visits of great multitudes of tourists, either on account of their real attractiveness, or because it is the fashion.

With this general view of the Falls, the reader will be prepared for the details, which, taken together, make up the comprehensive whole, and which constitute a visit to Niagara an event replete with lasting memories.

It detracts not a little from the enjoyment of the spectator to find that at this resort the oriental demand for "backsheesh" prevails in the modified form of tolls, fees, etc., and that what is here enjoyed in the line of sight-seeing must be paid for. Yet this is not to be wondered at when we consider that the parties who own the vantage ground must thus reap from it a sustaining harvest. What is legitimately demanded of the visitor in the way of tolls and admission fees may be considered as a *sine qua non*, and should not in the least mar his pleasure, as he receives in such cases a full equivalent for his expenditure.

"TRICKS THAT ARE [NOT ALWAYS] VAIN."

There is one thing, however, which no tourist is prepared to meet with composure, and which he will need to guard against here, namely, extortion, or an unexpected or unreasonable demand for money in payment for services not contracted for nor supposed to be in the market. Much has been said and written about the extortions of Niagara hackmen, until their practices have become a byword. In justice to some of these individuals it should be said that there are among them honorable men, who will do by you just as they agree, and will make no effort to defraud. It is always safe, however, to make an agreement with your driver as to the service he is to render you, and just what you are to pay him in return. When the terms of your contract are met, *accept no further service without understanding its cost.*

The need of this precaution will be apparent from the following facts. The lawful rate for carrying a passenger from one point to another in the villages about the Falls is fifty cents, or one dollar from village to village; yet a driver will frequently offer to carry a passenger for *ten cents.* Once in the carriage, however, he is urged to see this and that point of interest, and with the memory of the ten-cent offer as a basis for prospective expenses, he often yields to the importunities of the hackman, until he finds to his dismay that he has run up a bill, by the legal tariff, of from three to five dollars. While the man is charging him only what the law allows him to collect, the victim is chagrined at the method by which it is extorted from him, and it rankles as an unpleasant memory in his otherwise pleasurable recollections of his visit.

HORSESHOE FALLS AND RAPIDS.

We have been thus explicit in treating upon a subject to which no Niagara guide book we have ever seen gives more than a passing allusion, in order that the tourist may know what to expect, and how to meet it in the very outset. If you choose to accept of a hackman's "ten-cent" offer, be sure that you take no more than is "nominated in the bond," lest with the "pound of flesh" there come a drop of blood more costly than all the rest.

THE FIRST VIEW OF THE FALLS.

The approach to Niagara, by the line of the Michigan Central, is by a route nearly parallel with the river, from above on the Canada shore, and is beyond question, the best view to be had from any railroad train conveying its passengers near the place. As the train draws near the mighty cataract, the foaming rapids above the Falls burst upon the view, as if to prepare the mind for the exhibition of resistless power to be revealed in the grand plunge of waters into the abyss below.

In a few moments the train comes to a halt in full view of the Falls, with the Horseshoe or Canada Fall in the foreground, and Goat Island and the American Fall directly across the river, with the deep gorge between through which the river flows, spanned by the new suspension bridge. The picture thus presented is one of surpassing beauty. While a nearer view will impress the mind more completely with the sublime majesty of the cataract, the comprehensive grouping here presented will linger in the mind of a true lover of the beautiful, prominent among the "pictures that hang on memory's wall."

The through passengers, who make no tarry at the Falls, remain in the cars until the train arrives at Suspension Bridge, two miles below, this arrangement continuing for the present season, until the completion of the new bridge now in process of erection by the Michigan Central Company. When this structure is completed, the trains will cross the river in full view of the Falls. This, in addition to the view now obtained from the train, will prove a strong attraction to through travelers, inducing them to come by this route.

NIAGARA FALLS, ONTARIO.

This village, formerly known as Clifton, extends along the Canada shore of Niagara River, from near the Falls to the railroad suspension bridge. The tourist who wishes to inspect the cataract first from the Canada side, leaves the train at Niagara Falls station; and should he choose to find a temporary abiding place on the Canada side, he will find several well-kept hotels, at prices varying according to accommodations desired. The largest and most commodious of these is the CLIFTON HOUSE, which has been open to the public for more than forty years, and has established a reputation as in all respects a first-class house.

THE PROSPECT HOUSE is almost on the very verge of the Falls, being located at Table Rock, and commands a fine view. The house has an excellent reputation, its patrons being among the most celebrated of the visitors, both from America and abroad.

The BRUNSWICK, located a little farther down the bank than the house just mentioned,—just far enough, the proprietor claims, to be free from the annoyance of mist and spray, but sufficiently near to give a beautiful prospect from its windows and balconies,—furnishes a pleasant stopping place, less pretentious than some of its larger rivals, but with all its appointments complete, and well calculated to promote the comfort of its patrons. It can take good care of large or small parties, and is indeed a desirable stopping place for those who wish to tarry for a single day, or for a longer period, the terms being moderate and the fare excellent.

AMERICAN FALL, AS SEEN FROM CANADA SIDE.

Other houses there are on this side, of which the limits of this work forbid even a mention. Indeed, the provisions for the care of tourists indicate that for a considerable portion of the year at least, that constitutes by far the largest business of the dwellers in the vicinity.

The Canada shore can claim one point over all other localities in the vicinity of the Falls, in being the only place where a good view of the cataract can be had without the payment of toll or admittance fees. The effort now being made to create a public park on the New York shore, and thus secure similar privileges in the "land of the free," is attracting much attention from tourists. Its results are as yet conjectural, but so much has the value of the property become enhanced by the very practices which this plan proposes to abolish, it seems now like a great undertaking to accomplish what a few years ago would have been much more easily brought about.

There are opportunities, however, to pay fees on the Canada side, and to receive an equivalent in return. A staircase leading to the foot of the Horseshoe Fall, permits a fine view from below, and in addition a visit to the cavernous recess under Table Rock and Horseshoe Fall. For the latter excursion, water-proof suits and the services of a guide are necessary, and the experience is one long to be remembered.

TABLE ROCK.

Table Rock itself is an object of much curiosity. It is an overhanging cliff, extending along the bank to the very junction with the Horseshoe Fall. Its shape and dimensions have been several times changed within the memory and observation of the present generation, and "the oldest inhabitants" remember it as projecting far beyond its present limits. In July, 1818, a mass some thirty or forty feet wide, and about one hundred and sixty feet in length, fell into the bed of the river. In December, 1828, three sections, comprising a very large portion of the overhanging cliff, and extending to the verge of the Horseshoe Fall, broke off and fell with a terrible crash. In the summer of 1829, another large mass separated and fell, and in June, 1850, still another, the latter about 60 feet wide by 200 long. The precipice still hangs far out over the perpendicular, and with these losses in view, the reader can readily imagine its appearance before the action of the elements had robbed it of so much that made it celebrated.

TABLE ROCK.

Several other objects of interest are to be seen on the Canada side, which will be mentioned further on in these pages, and we will now proceed to a description of the principal objects of interest immediately connected with the Falls. In crossing the river to the American shore, the visitor has a choice of two methods. He may descend the bank and cross by the ferry, or may go over the New Suspension Bridge. If intending to return, he will do well to go over by the bridge and re-cross by the ferry.

THE NEW SUSPENSION BRIDGE.

This structure, although opened to the public in 1869, is still called the *new* bridge, to distinguish it from its elder brother, two miles below. Previous to the construction of the New York and Brooklyn bridge, it was the longest suspension bridge in the world, its roadway being 1,300 feet in length, and its cables 1,800 feet long. It is 190 feet above the river, being suspended from two towers, each 100 feet in height. Access may be had to the interior of the towers, and very fine views are obtained from their summits.

From the bridge itself a magnificent view of the Falls may be had, the finest, in fact, to be secured from any one point, the entire line of the cataract being embraced in a single glance, and in closer proximity than is possible elsewhere, except from below. The view down the river is also a fine one, comprising the deep gorge through which the stream flows, with its precipitous banks on either hand, and the Railroad Suspension Bridge in the distance.

The strength of the new bridge is estimated by the engineers as thirteen times greater than sufficient to bear any weight that can possibly be placed upon it. The year of its completion it was subjected to the severest gale it has ever had to withstand, and safely and successfully "weathered the blast." All fears, therefore, as to its security in ordinary weather, are entirely groundless.

Reaching the American shore by this method of crossing, the first point of interest is

PROSPECT PARK.

Depositing the fee of 25 cents at the toll-gate, we are soon within the privileged domain. The grounds are what were formerly known as the "Ferry Grove" and "Point View," and previous to their improvement were free to the public. The Company who purchased them, however, have provided an almost endless variety of artificial adjuncts to render the place attractive, and the small fee exacted for admission is not, therefore, an unreasonable one.

At the verge of the American Fall, they have constructed a solid wall at what is now called "Prospect Point," extending it all along the brink of the precipice, thus rendering secure from accident the place where the finest view of the Fall can be obtained. Looking up the stream, the foaming rapids, white-crested and tumultuous, greet the vision in a continuous stretch, until water and sky seem to blend. In the immediate foreground is the American Fall, its waters almost in reach of the outstretched hand. Directly across the stream are Luna and Goat Islands, while sweeping away to the right in a grand curve, is the Horseshoe Fall. The American Fall is year by year assuming the horseshoe form, by the wearing away of the cliff in the center, the indentation in the front line of the Fall being quite prominently visible from Prospect Point, although less noticeable from a front view.

VIEW OF THE FALLS FROM THE FERRY.

The visitor who may be disposed to carry away a souvenir of this locality will find a skillful photographer in readiness to make pictures, stereoscopic or otherwise, of from one to twenty persons, with both the American and the Horseshoe Fall as a background.

Near the Point is located a bazaar for the sale of curiosities, in itself a museum well worthy of a visit, whether to purchase be the intention, or only to inspect the articles exposed for sale.

The Ferry House is near the center of the Park, and is the upper terminal station of the

INCLINED PLANE RAILWAY.

A tunnel has been cut from the cliff to the margin of the river, at an angle of about thirty degrees, and within it is built the railway, by the side of which is a flight of stairs, numbering 290 steps. The cars are raised and lowered by machinery, operated by a turbine wheel, and are so arranged that one ascends while the other descends. This railway has been in successful operation, without a casualty, for nearly forty years. The timid, however, to whom the descent appears perilous, have the choice of the stairway for reaching the river, and many prefer to trust their own limbs in the climb, but are generally glad to avail themselves of the car in returning. At the foot of the stairs, a commodious building has been erected, from which a view of the Falls from below may be had through windows which protect the visitor from the spray. A nearer view may be obtained by donning a water-proof suit, for which facilities are provided in the dressing-rooms, and, with a trusty guide, taking a promenade upon "Hurricane Bridge," at the very foot of the American Fall, completing the trip by going *behind* the cataract itself, which may be done in safety, and constitutes a novel experience. The cavernous recess behind the curtain of falling water extends nearly to the center of the Fall, and is filled with the dashing spray which perpetually rises from the cauldron of waters. The roar of the cataract echoes and re-echoes within this chamber, the effect being heightened by the compression of the air; and the combined effect upon the senses as one thus stands as it were within the very grasp of Nature's most powerful forces, serves to show the contrast between puny man and his omnipotent Creator.

Between the foot of the Inclined Plane and the Canada shore, a line of ferry boats has been established, affording a safe and pleasant method of transit between those points, and a view of the Falls from the river level. The best time for this trip is early in the morning or an hour or two before sunset, and the impressions made upon the mind in connection with it, will be among the most lasting of all the recollections of Niagara.

Returning to the Park by the stairway or the car, as the traveler may elect, we continue our examination of the objects of interest to be found within its limits. Its shady groves and pleasant walks, remnants of the natural forest improved by the hand of art, furnish delightful resting places or promenades; and its Art Gallery, Concert Hall, Pavilion, and other provisions for entertainment, serve to engage the attention of the visitor, and make pleasant the hours that pass while within the Park.

ELECTRIC ILLUMINATION.

One of the most enjoyable features of the visit to Prospect Park is that provided for the hours of evening. The illumination of the Falls and fountains by the electric light is a pleasing spectacle, and well worthy of a tarry to see. The electricity for the purpose is developed by one of the largest sized dynamo machines, kept in operation by a powerful turbine wheel, located in the Ferry building, the water-power supplied by a canal. The brilliant light thus produced is concentrated upon the Falls and Rapids, both in clear white and with prismatic effects, rendering them even more beautiful by night than in the full light of day.

An arrangement of fountains in which the waters are made to assume a variety of shapes, with revolving wheels and jets of spray, the whole illuminated with shifting lights of all colors, constitutes an exhibition amply rewarding a long journey to behold. The observer is fascinated by the ever-changing colors and gorgeous effects, more beautiful than any pyrotechnic display, which it very much resembles, only with intensified brilliancy of coloring, and more enduring in form.

GOAT ISLAND.

Passing out at the gate of Prospect Park, a short walk brings us to the toll-house of Goat Island, at the end of the bridge leading across to the group of islands which divide the cataract into its two distinctive parts. The largest of these bears the above name, which was given to it from a trivial circumstance, illustrating how easily a nickname or title becomes fastened "to stay" with a few repetitions, even from an unauthorized source. More than a century ago, a Mr. John Stedman placed some goats on the upper end of the Island, and through neglect they were suffered to remain uncared for during the winter, and died from exposure. Hence the name, which adheres to it, in preference to its authorized name of "Iris Island."

The group comprises, in all, some seventeen islands, large and small, covering about sixty acres. The property belongs to the estate of the late Judge Porter, to whom it was ceded by the State of New York in 1818. Its possession at that time was regarded as of little consequence, and the attempt to put a bridge across was deemed foolhardiness; but it is said that an offer of a million and a half dollars has recently been refused for the estate.

GOAT-ISLAND BRIDGE.

The first bridge was a frail structure, and was soon carried away. It was replaced by a stronger one, which stood from 1818 to 1856, when it was removed, and the present elegant structure substituted. The foundations are heavy oaken cribs, filled with stone and plated with iron. The bridge itself is of iron, in four arches, each of ninety feet span, making a total length of three hundred and sixty feet. Its width is twenty-seven feet, comprising a double carriageway, with footway on either side. The bridge is a favorite place from which to view the Rapids, as the waters near the precipice below.

The first island of the group is Bath Island, which is utilized as the site of manufacturing enterprise, a large paper-mill occupying a position to command some portion of the splendid water-power so idly expending itself for naught. Crossing by a bridge of a single span to Goat Island, we find ourselves in a spot where Nature has been comparatively undisturbed. The forest remains almost in its primeval simplicity, which fact renders this a most charming and popular resort. Indeed, a visit to Niagara would be sadly incomplete were Goat Island and its attractions to be omitted.

Ascending a slight rise from the bridge, the road leads into a shady forest, and branches in three directions. The best method of visiting the points of interest is to first turn to the right, and follow the road or path to the foot of the Island, emerging from the forest near the stairway and bridge leading to

LUNA ISLAND.

This small but pleasant little islet divides the American Fall into two sections, the stream over which we cross from Goat Island constituting what is known as the Center Fall, beneath which is the Cave of the Winds. The island lies low, and the visitor may touch the water with the hand. The verge was formerly unguarded, but an iron railing now prevents a repetition of the melancholy accident that occurred here on the 21st of June, 1849, when the family of Mr. Deforest, of Buffalo, in company with a friend, Mr. Charles Addington, were visiting the scene. The latter, playfully catching up Annette, the little daughter of Mr. Deforest, said, "I am going to throw you in." With a sudden impulse, the child sprang from his arms into the water. Horrified at the result of his pleasantry, Mr. Addington sprang after her, and both were immediately carried over the Falls. The mangled remains of the child were recovered the same day, in the Cave of the Winds, and the body of the unfortunate young man a few days later.

Returning to Goat Island, a short walk brings us to the building used as the dressing-room in which to prepare for a visit to the

"CAVE OF THE WINDS."

This trip is made by ladies as well as gentlemen, water-proof suits being provided for any who wish to explore the famous cavern, and experienced guides are in readiness to accompany the visitor. The descent to the foot of the cliff is here made without the aid of machinery, by means of a spiral staircase known as

"BIDDLE'S STAIRS."

This structure takes its name from the Hon. Nicholas Biddle, the well-known president of the United States Bank, at whose expense the enterprise of building it was carried out in 1829. The bank at this place is 185 feet high. Part of this descent is accomplished by an open stairway, of ordinary inclination, and the remainder by the perpendicular shaft or tower, which is 80 feet high, the whole comprising 147 steps.

UNDER THE CATARACT.

From the foot of the tower, a pathway to the right, under the shadow of the overhanging cliff, leads to the Center Fall, which constitutes the aqueous curtain of "Æolus' Cavern." A secure stairway leads to the entrance of the Cave, and the visitor passes under the Fall, into the stormy recess made in the solid rock. The Cavern derives its name from the peculiar atmospheric effects produced by the action of the falling water, the compression of the air establishing a perpetual tempest, like that in which Æolus, the god of the wind, is said to dwell.

The Cave is 100 feet high by 100 deep and 160 long, and its existence is due to the action of the waters upon the shale, leaving the more solid limestone rock overhanging.

As one of the many novel experiences to be met in a visit to Niagara, the trip through this Cave will leave a lasting impression upon the memory. The sensations which wind and storm will always produce are here intensified by the novelty of the surroundings, and the realization of the fact that the forces of Nature are perpetually accomplishing here what they occasionally produce in the outer world. Add to this the spice of personal risk, really less than it seems to be, and the recollections of the occasion will be vivid and enduring.

From the foot of the stairway, another path leads to the river in front, and still another toward the Canadian or Horseshoe Fall. The latter is but little used, and is not kept in good condition. From a scaffolding 100 feet high, erected near the stairway in 1829, Sam Patch made his famous leap into the river, successfully accomplishing a feat, the repetition of which at Genessee Falls, shortly after, cost him his life.

Returning to the bank above, and continuing the walk along the brink, the next interesting point of observation is

TERRAPIN BRIDGE AND ROCK.

A stairway leads down to the Bridge, which crosses over to the Rock where for forty years the well-known Terrapin Tower constituted a landmark to be seen from all directions, standing as it did at the very verge of the Falls. The rock itself furnishes a favorable outlook, affording a near view of the Horseshoe Fall. The bridge is liable to be slippery from the action of the spray, and care should be exercised to avoid accident. In the winter of 1852, a gentleman while in the act of crossing fell into the stream, and was carried to the very verge of the Fall. By a remarkably fortunate circumstance, he lodged between two rocks, when he was discovered by some of the citizens, who rescued him by life lines, which he succeeded in fastening around his body. He was carried to a hotel, and remained speechless for several hours, so great was the shock to his nervous system.

THE CANADIAN OR HORSESHOE FALL,

Which is here seen to the best advantage, is about 144 rods wide, and 158 feet high. The depth of the water in the center is estimated at 20 feet. An experiment to demonstrate the depth was made in 1827. An unseaworthy vessel, drawing 18 feet of water, increased by leakage to more than 20 feet, was sent over the Falls, and cleared the ledge without touching.

The name "Horseshoe" is hardly true to the present shape, which is now more nearly rectangular. The horseshoe curve has been marred by the falling of portions of the cliff at various times, until its original symmetry has nearly departed. The precipice near the Terrapin Tower has suffered loss from this cause, until it was regarded as unsafe to continue the use of the Tower, and it was removed in 1873.

TERRAPIN TOWER.—REMOVED IN 1873.

Along the south shore of the island, the walk or drive toward the east keeps in view the rapids, and leads us next to the group known as the

THREE SISTER ISLANDS.

These are connected with Goat Island and with one another by three hand-some bridges, affording a magnificent view of the Rapids, the best, in fact, to be had from any point of observation. The scene presented from the outer island, as you gaze up the river, upon the vast expanse of foaming, turbulent water, seemingly threatening to overwhelm you and the ground on which you stand, and yet dividing as it passes you, or abating its fury as it reaches the shore at your feet, is one to fill the soul with admiration and awe, as, perhaps, no other view can do. The outlook from the bridges also awakens peculiar emotions. Standing only a few feet above the rapidly coursing torrent as it passes beneath you, the thought comes to the mind that here at least, "there is but a step betwixt time and eternity." The fascination increases as the gaze is prolonged, and the mind which cannot be impressed with the sublimity of the scene, must be, like the soul devoid of music, "fit for treason, stratagem, and spoils."

At the head of Goat Island, a little farther up the river, the view is quite expansive, commanding both banks of the stream, and the islands in the channel. Beginning at the right, the site of Fort Schlosser is seen about a mile away, marked by a small white building and a very large chimney. The name is associated with border history, the fort having been built by the French, afterward ceded to the English, and occupied as a military station by Captain Schlosser, from whom its later name was derived, the French having given it the title of Little Fort.

NAVY ISLAND,

Lying in the channel which sweeps around Grand Island on the Canada side, has an area of over three hundred acres, and is associated with Fort Schlosser in the annals of border history, having been made the *rendezvous* of the "Patriots" in the "Rebellion" of 1837, under the leadership of McKenzie, who, with about twenty-five or thirty followers, became disaffected with the Canadian authorities, and planted their standard here as a rallying-point. The American steamer Caroline, a small boat supposed to be in the service of the "Rebels," was chartered to run between the islands and the American shore. Friday, Dec. 29, 1837, she entered upon her work of "ferriage," and after a profitable day's work was moved to the wharf at Schlosser's Landing. The same night, a detachment of British soldiers, under command of Capt. Drew, seized her, set her on fire, and the little steamer went down the stream in flames, and plunged over the Canadian Fall. The crew, and some of the "patriots" who were on board, escaped to the shore, with the exception of one man, Durfee, who was killed by a pistol shot in attempting to escape.

GRAND ISLAND,

The largest in the River Niagara, is twelve miles in length, its breadth varying from two to seven miles. Its soil, unlike that of the islands nearer the cataract, is very fertile, and much of it is under cultivation. Its historic annals are less interesting than those just mentioned, although one enterprise has a monumental reminder, still in a good state of preservation. A gentleman who in the current vernacular of to-day would doubtless be entitled a "crank," conceived the project of making this island a place of refuge for the scattered tribes of Israel. In 1825 he laid the corner-stone of the "City of Ararat," and erected a monument with imposing ceremonies. The latter still serves to remind the visitor that "cranks" are not original with the present generation.

At the foot of Grand Island is a smaller one, of about three hundred acres, called Buckhorn Island. The channel between them is called "Burnt Ship Bay," from the destruction of two armed supply vessels by the French garrison at Schlosser, near the close of the French war of 1759, to prevent their acquisition by the English. They were brought to this bay, and set on fire, and the circumstance is thus commemorated by the name of the bay.

Corner's Island, Gill Creek Island and Grass Island, all of them small, lie near the American shore, and are important, commercially or historically.

FATHER HENNEPIN'S SKETCH OF THE FALLS.

The first white man who saw the Falls, of whom we have any account, was Father Hennepin, the noted explorer. We present above a *fac-simile* of the sketch made by him, representing the Falls as they were 200 years ago. We also give his extravagant description, preserving the orthography and the quaint style in which it was written:—

"Betwixt the Lake *Ontario* and *Erie*, there is a vast and prodigious Cadence of Water which falls down after a surprizing and astonishing manner, insomuch that the Universe does not afford its Parallel. 'Tis true, *Italy* and *Suedeland* boast of some such Things; but we may well say they are but sorry Patterns, when compar'd to this of which we now speak. At the foot of this horrible Precipice, we meet with the River *Niagara*, which is not above a quarter of a League broad, but is wonderfully deep in some places. It is so rapid above this Descent, that it violently hurries down the wild Beasts while endeavoring to pass it to feed on the other side, they not being able to withstand the force of its Current, which inevitably casts them headlong above Six hundred foot high.

"This wonderful Downfal is compounded of two great Cross-streams of Water, and two Falls, with an Isle sloping along the middle of it. The Waters which fall from this horrible Precipice, do foam and boyl after the most hideous manner imaginable, making an outrageous Noise, more terrible than that of Thunder; for when the Wind blows out of the South, their dismal roaring may be heard more than Fifteen Leagues off.

"The River *Niagara* having thrown it self down this incredible Precepice, continues its impetuous course for two Leagues together, to the great Rock above-mention'd, with an inexpressible rapidity: But having past that, its impetuosity relents, gliding along more gently for other two Leagues, till it arrive at the Lake *Ontario* or *Frontenac*.

"Any Bark or greater Vessel may pass from the Fort to the foot of this huge Rock above-mention'd. This Rock lies to the Westward, and is cut off from the Land by the River *Niagara*, about two Leagues farther down than the great Fall; for which two Leagues the People are oblig'd to transport their Goods over-land; but the way is very good; and the Trees are but few, chiefly Firrs and Oaks.

"From the great Fall unto this Rock which is to the West of the River, the two Brinks of it are so prodigious high, that it would make one tremble to look steadily upon the Water, rolling along with a rapidity not to be imagin'd. Were it not for this vast Cataract, which interrupts Navigation, they might fail with Barks or greater Vessels, more than Four hundred and fifty Leagues, crossing the Lake of *Hurons*, and reaching even to the farther end of the Lake *Illinois*; which two Lakes we may easily say are little Seas of fresh Water."

RETROCESSION OF THE FALLS.

The following extracts from an article written by Prof. Tyndall will be of interest in this connection:—

"The fact that in historic times, even within the memory of man, the Fall has sensibly receded, prompts the question, How far has this recession gone? At what point did the ledge which thus continually creeps backward begin its retrograde course? To minds disciplined in such researches the answer has been and will be, At the precipitous declivity which crosses the Niagara from Lewiston on the American to Queenston on the Canadian side. Over this traverse barrier the affluents of all upper lakes once poured their waters, and here the work of erosion began. The dam, moreover, was demonstrably of sufficient height to cause the river above it to submerge Goat Island, and this would perfectly account for the finding by Mr. Hall, Sir Charles Lyell, and others, in the sand and gravel of the island, the same fluviatile shells as are now found in the Niagara River higher up. It would also account for those deposits along the sides of the river, the discovery of which enabled Lyell, Hall, and Ramsay to reduce to demonstration the popular belief that the Niagara once flowed through a shallow valley.

"The physics of the problem of excavation, which I made clear to my mind before quitting Niagara, are revealed by a close inspection of the present Horseshoe Fall. Here we see evidently that the greatest weight of water bends over the very apex of the Horseshoe. In a passage in his excellent chapter on Niagara Falls, Mr. Hall alludes to this fact. Here we have the most copious and the most violent whirling of the shattered liquid; here the most powerful eddies recoil against the shale. From this portion of the Fall, indeed, the spray sometimes rises without solution of continuity to the region of clouds, becoming gradually more attenuated, and passing finally through the condition of true cloud into invisible vapor, which is sometimes re-precipitated higher up. All the phenomena point distinctly to the center of the river as the place of the greatest mechanical energy, and from the center the vigor of the Fall gradually dies away toward the sides. The horseshoe form, with the concavity facing downward, is an obvious and necessary consequence of this action. Right along the middle of the river the apex of the curve pushes its way backward, cutting along the center a deep and comparatively narrow groove, and draining the sides as it passes them. Hence the remarkable discrepancy between the widths of the Niagara above and below the Horseshoe. All along its course, from Lewiston Heights to the present position, the form of the Fall was probably that of a horseshoe; for this is merely the expression of the greater depth, and consequently greater excavating power, of the center of the river. The gorge, moreover, varies in width as the depth, of the center of the ancient river varied, being narrowest where that depth was greatest.

"The vast comparative erosive energy of the Horseshoe Fall comes strikingly into view when it and the American Fall are compared together. The American branch of the upper river is cut at a right angle by the gorge of the Niagara. Here the Horseshoe Fall was the real excavator. It cut the rock, and formed the precipice over which the American Fall tumbles. But since its formation the erosive action of the American Fall has been almost *nil*, while the Horseshoe has cut its way for five hundred yards across the end of Goat Island, and is now doubling back to excavate a channel parallel to the length of the island. This point, I have just learned, has not escaped the acute observation of Prof. Ramsay. The river bends; the Horseshoe immediately accommodates itself to the bending, and will follow implicitly the direction of the deepest water in the upper stream. The flexibility of the gorge, if I may use the term, is determined by the flexibility of the river channel above it. Were the Niagara above the Fall sinuous, the gorge would immediately follow its sinuosities. Once suggested, no doubt geographers will be able to point out many examples of this action. The Zambesi is thought to present a great difficulty to the erosion theory, because of the sinuosity of the chasm below the Victoria Falls. But assuming the basalt to be of tolerably uniform texture, had the river been examined before the formation of this sinuous channel, the present zigzag course of the gorge below the Fall could, I am persuaded, have been predicted, while the sounding of the present river would enable us to predict the course to be pursued by the erosion in the future.

"But not only has the Niagara River cut the gorge—it has carried away the chips of its own workshop. The shale being probably crumbled, is easily carried away. But at the base of the Fall we find the huge boulders already described, and by some means or other these are removed down the river. The ice which tills the gorge in winter, and which grapples with the boulders, has been regarded as the transporting agent. Probably it is so to some extent. But erosion acts without ceasing on the abutting points of the boulder, thus withdrawing their support, and urging them down the river. Solution also does its portion of the work. That solid matter is carried down is proved by the difference of depth between the Niagara River and Lake Ontario, where the river enters it. The depth falls from seventy-two feet to twenty feet, in consequence of the deposition of solid matter caused by the diminished motion of the river. Near the mouth of the gorge at Queenston, the depth, according to the Admiralty Chart, is 180 feet; well within the gorge, it is 132 feet."

SUSPENSION BRIDGE.

Two miles below the Falls, the river is spanned by the structure so widely known by the above name. The banks are here very precipitous, and the river deep and rapid, and the erection of piers in the stream being an impossibility, the structure is suspended from cables passing over towers of solid masonry. The following statistics will be of interest to those of our readers who revel in figures:—

Length of span from center to center of towers	822	feet.
Height of tower above rock on the American side	88	feet.
Height of tower above rock on the Canada side	78	feet.
Height of tower above floor of railway	60	feet.
Height of track above water	258	feet.
Number of wire cables	4	
Diameter of each cable	10 ½	in.
Number of No. 9 wires in each cable	3,659	
Ultimate aggregate strength of cables	12,400	feet.
Weight of superstructure	800	feet.
Weight of superstructure and maximum loads	1,250	feet.
Maximum weight the cable and stays will support	7,309	feet.

The bridge is a "two-story" affair, the upper part being used for the railway, and the lower for carriages and foot passengers.

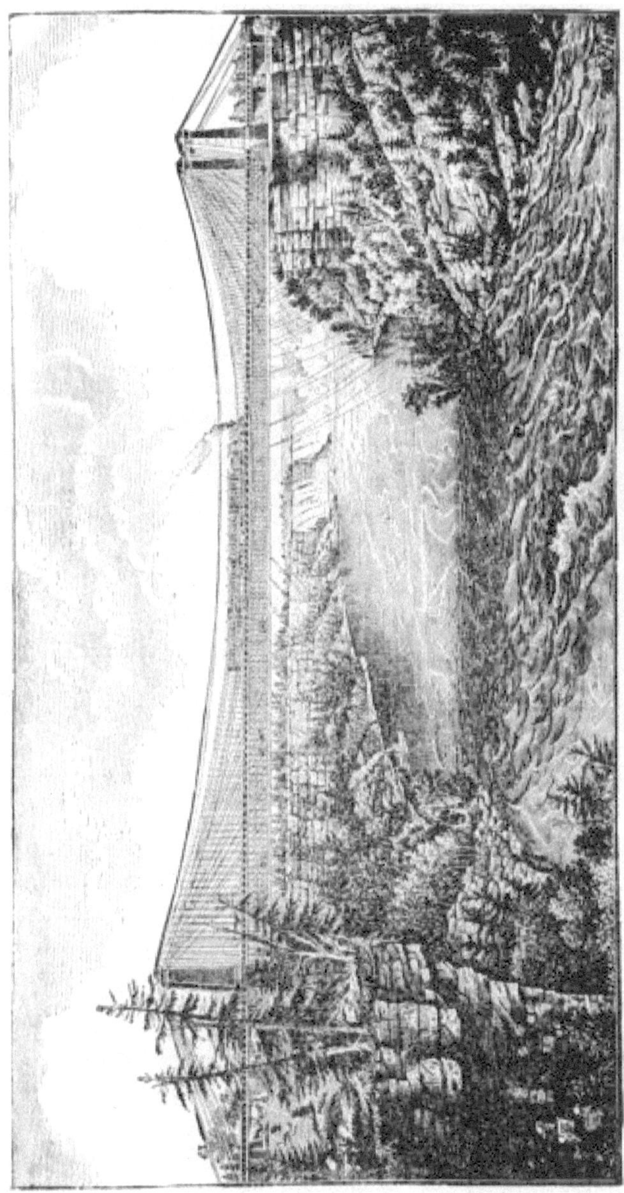

RAILWAY SUSPENSION BRIDGE, NIAGARA RIVER.

WHIRLPOOL RAPIDS.

The narrowing of the channel in the vicinity of the Suspension Bridge greatly accelerates the current, and the tremendous force with which it rushes through the gorge from this point to the "Whirlpool," throws the water into violent commotion. When it is considered that the calculated weight of the water that passes over the Falls every hour is 100,000,000 tons, and that this volume of water must find its way through a channel only about 300 feet wide, the terrific force with which it rushes along may be at least partially understood. Although the depth of the stream is here estimated at 250 feet, the force of the current is such as to *elevate* the water from ten to forty feet above its natural level.

WHIRLPOOL AND RAPIDS.

At the Whirlpool, the river takes a sharp turn almost at a right angle, circling around in the cauldron which it seems to have excavated for itself, and finally making its exit through a narrow gorge, the vast body of water no doubt passing out far below the surface, in a channel of immense depth.

The Whirlpool may be seen to advantage from either the Canadian or the American side. At the latter, the approach is through the grounds of De Veaux College, the fee for admission going to the funds of the institution. On the Canada side, extensive preparations have been made for the accommodation of visitors by the WHIRLPOOL RAPIDS PARK COMPANY.

A river-side walk has been constructed, partially by excavation from the side of the cliff, and a delightful park on the bank of the river, with plenty of trees and shrubbery, renders a promenade on this shore very attractive. An inclined railway, to facilitate the journey between the upper and lower levels, has been constructed, and equipped with cars, operating in a novel and ingenious manner. The cars have tanks below the seats; these tanks are filled with water from a spring at the back of the entrance building, by means of a pipe leading into the tank. 50 lbs. weight of water is sufficient to overcome the balance of the cars, and to carry the loaded car to the foot of the railway, the light one being simultaneously drawn to the top by the same power. Formerly these cars were operated by steam-power, but the present is by far the safest and most economical plan, there being no machinery to get out of order, no danger of damage from bursting of boiler, etc., the entire apparatus necessary being the check or governor, by which the person in charge can regulate or stop the speed of the car with perfect ease. These cars take 12 passengers each; the tanks are capable of containing 2,800 lbs. of water. As they reach the foot of the incline, a bolt or pin removes the fastening to the discharge pipe and discharges the water, thus leaving the car in readiness for its next ascent, which is made in about one and a half minutes. The total length of the railroad is 285 feet.

At the water's edge, a photographic studio is located, thus giving to all an opportunity of being portrayed with the Whirlpool Rapids in the backgrounds.

Returning again to the Falls, we find on the Canada side several points of interest, not yet considered in these pages. At Table Rock an opportunity is afforded of visiting the MUSEUM, a collection of natural curiosities, works of art, etc., well worthy of a visit. A zoological garden is kept in connection, and an observatory affords a good outlook from a lofty stand-point.

THE BURNING SPRING.

About a mile above the Falls, reached by a pleasant drive or walk, across Cedar Island, in view of the Rapids, is the natural curiosity known as the Burning Spring, the waters of which are highly charged with sulphuretted hydrogen, which burns with a pale blue flame when ignited. This is supposed to have its origin in a coal formation, believed by some to be extensive, and worthy of mining. The proprietor, however, has not sufficient faith in the feasibility of the scheme to undertake it. Clark Hill Islands, a group of five, which are crossed in the approach to the burning spring, are in the midst of the rapids, and a fine carriage drive extends along their outer shores, affording a good view of the current, which is here very rapid. These islands are connected with the main land by two suspension bridges, which have been named "Castor" and "Pollux."

On Cedar Island, near the Horseshoe Falls, a Pagoda has been erected, over 80 feet in height, from which a magnificent view can be had. It is a noticeable landmark from all points in the vicinity of the Falls.

LUNDY'S LANE BATTLE FIELD.

As a spot, of no little historical interest, the scene of the decisive battle between the English and American forces, July 25, 1814, receives many visitors, of all nationalities. The ground is about a mile and a half due west from the Falls, near the village of Drummondville, named in honor of Gen. Drummond, who commanded the British forces in the engagement. Two towers have been erected to mark the spot, and from their summits a good view is had of the surrounding country. It was the writer's good fortune, on the occasion of his first visit to the scene, some years ago, to listen to a description of the battle from the lips of a surviving participant, who wore the British uniform on the occasion, but who gave the American forces great credit for gallantry in the fight. The total loss, in killed and wounded, was about eighteen hundred men.

DEVIL'S HOLE.

About half a mile below the Whirlpool, on the American side, a gloomy cavern in the bank has received the above title. It is about one hundred feet in depth, and from its forbidding aspect might well be regarded as the property of his Satanic majesty. Tradition makes this locality the scene of the massacre of the English supply train and escort in 1763, by the Seneca Indians, instigated by the French traders. The train was on its way from Fort Niagara to Fort Schlosser, and only three of its number escaped alive, while of the escort only eight returned to Fort Niagara.

NIAGARA RIVER BELOW THE WHIRLPOOL.

Much that would be of interest to the reader might be written concerning the Falls and the surroundings, but we have already devoted a large amount of space to the subject, and must close with a few necessary particulars. For the convenience of those who may need the facts, we tabulate the rates of toll, carriage hire, etc., the latter being the rate fixed by law as permissible. It may be well to add, however, that most of the drivers are willing to make a special rate, considerably lower than those given, and, as previously remarked, this should be expressly agreed upon before starting out, including an understanding as to the payment of the tolls and gate fees.

RATES OF TOLL

Goat Island	$ .50
Cave of the Winds	1.00
Prospect Park	.25
Inclined Railway	.25
Shadow of the Rock	1.00

New Suspension Bridge	.25
Ferry	.25
Behind Sheet of Water (Table Rock)	1.00
Burning Spring	.50
Railway Bridge, over and back	.50
Whirlpool Rapids	.50
Whirlpool	.50

RATES OF FARE ALLOWED BY LAW,

FOR CARRIAGE HIRE WHERE NO EXPRESS CONTRACT IS MADE THEREFOR.

For carrying one passenger and ordinary baggage from one place to another in the village, 50 cents.

Each additional passenger and ordinary baggage, 25 cents.

For carrying one passenger and ordinary baggage from any point in this village to any point in the village of Suspension Bridge, 1 dollar.

Each additional passenger and ordinary baggage, 50 cents.

Each additional piece of baggage other than ordinary baggage, 12 cents.

Children under 3 years of age, free.

Over 3 years and under 14 years, half price.

Ordinary baggage is defined to be 1 trunk and 1 bag, hat or band-box, or other small parcel.

For carrying one or more passengers, in the same carriage, from any point in this village to any point within 5 miles of the limits of the village, at the rate of $1.50 for each hour occupied, except that in every instance where such carriage shall be drawn by a single horse, the fare therefor shall be at the rate of 1 dollar for each hour occupied.

HOTELS.—Although a little out of its natural connection, this subject seems to demand at least a paragraph. The constant influx of visitors, especially during the summer months has created a demand for hotel accommodations at Niagara, which has been met in the erection of such houses as the Cataract, International, Spencer, Niagara, Kaltenbach, Goat Island, and a multitude of others, of various grades of excellence, both at the Falls and Suspension Bridge.

THE ST. LAWRENCE RIVER.

The route to the sea *via* the St. Lawrence River having become a great favorite with summer tourists, we give in this connection a description of some of its principal attractions. The majestic river, whose channel is the outlet for all the waters of the great chain of inland seas, runs in a general northeasterly direction, from Lake Ontario to the Gulf of St. Lawrence, through a country full of objects of interest to the traveler and sight-seer, and by its navigability becomes the medium by which they may be reached.

Leaving Niagara Falls in the evening, sleeping cars are run, *via* New York Central, Rome, Watertown & Ogdensburg, and Utica & Black River Railroads, to Clayton, arriving next morning in time to connect with the palace day steamers of the ST. LAWRENCE STEAMBOAT COMPANY. Should the tourist prefer to make the trip by daylight, he will find the scenery pleasant and attractive. He will thus reach Clayton in the evening, and remain until morning, proceeding as above.

The pleasures of a trip down the St. Lawrence, among the celebrated Thousand Islands, through the foaming rapids, and past the charming villages which lie along the shore, have been the theme of extravagant praise from many a summer tourist, and the constantly increasing popularity of this route is ample evidence that they do not soon grow old. You may usually find among the passengers many who have made the trip several seasons in succession, and the summer resorts of the St. Lawrence are visited by the same tourists year after year, so many and varied are the charms presented.

STEAMER ROTHESAY, "AMERICAN LINE."

LAKE OF THE THOUSAND ISLANDS.

CLAYTON, the steamboat landing of the AMERICAN LINE, is upon the shore of the river where it broadens out among the group of islands of nearly double the number indicated by the name. The trip therefore commences in the midst of beautiful scenery, to continue in a succession of delights and surprises, until its close at the wharf in Montreal. One and a half miles from Clayton is Round Island Park, occupying the island from which it takes its name. A lovelier spot is not to be found. An elegant hotel, numerous cottages, pleasant groves, splendid drives, and a beautiful water-front, are among the features that contribute to its attractiveness, and give promise of making it the resort *par excellence* among the island gems of this beautiful river. The association controlling the Park, while supposed to be denominational, is by no means sectarian, and the largest freedom is allowed the occupants, untrammeled by the claims or caprices of fashion, such as sometimes destroy all liberty at fashionable resorts.

THE LUXURY OF CAMP-LIFE.

Is here enjoyed to its fullest extent. The beautiful groves along the shores of the island, reached by boat or the inland paths and drives, afford delightful camping-places, while the ready communication with the "haunts of civilization" places the conveniences, and even luxuries for those who desire them, within easy reach.

Round Island is about a mile in length, and eight hundred to twelve hundred feet wide. Its shape is not correctly indicated by its name, it being more nearly oval than round.

ROUND ISLAND HOUSE.

In summing up the attractions of the island, we can do no better than to employ the language of one of its summer residents, who writes as follows:—

What Round Island has NOT: Marshes, mosquitoes, malaria, drinking saloons, accumulated refuse, impure air, impure water.

What Round Island has: The purest and most invigorating air, the clearest and most delicious water, the pleasantest drives, inviting walks, beautiful views, unparalleled scenery, facilities for amusement, accommodations for rest, cleanliness, healthfulness, between thirty and forty cottages, an elegant hotel, fifty-five acres of lawn, a two-mile driving track, bathing houses, and every convenience to make cottage or hotel life charming.

THOUSAND ISLAND PARK.

More widely known, perhaps, than any of the other St. Lawrence resorts, is the great camp-meeting park of the Methodist denomination bearing the above title. It is located at the upper end of Wells Island, and has rapidly grown to large proportions, combining, as it does, the religious, social and pleasure-seeking elements, often united in the same individuals. It has a large village of permanent cottages, which is greatly increased in the summer by the "cotton houses" of those who come for a brief stay, either in attendance upon the religious services or for a short respite from business in camp life. It has a post-office, public buildings, stores, and the conveniences of town life, together with boat houses, landings, dock room, etc., and being in the main channel of the river, it is readily accessible to visitors, as the boats make it one of their important landings.

WESTMINSTER PARK.

The lower portion of Wells Island is also under the control of a religious association, being owned by a regularly chartered society called the Westminster Park Association. With the usual conservatism of people of the "orthodox" faith, there is nothing of the camp-meeting order here, although services are held in Bethune chapel every Sunday during the season. The Park comprises about five hundred acres, occupying an irregular neck of upland, rising in some places to a commanding height, overlooking the scene for miles in extent. Tasteful cottages occupy the building lots into which a large portion of the Park has been divided. An elegant hotel, called the WESTMINSTER, under excellent management, is kept in first-class style, at from two to three dollars per day. Directly opposite from this park, on the New York shore, is

ALEXANDRIA BAY,

Sometimes called the "Saratoga of the St. Lawrence." As a summer resort, it is fairly entitled to the name, being one of the most popular watering places in America. Its summer hotels are among the most commodious and attractive to be found anywhere, while private cottages and villas have sprung up on every available site, both on the shore, and on all the islands near. The facilities for fishing and boating, combined with the pure and invigorating atmosphere, and the beautiful scenery, attract to the place a tide of summer visitors, ever increasing in volume with each succeeding year. Alexandria Bay is only twelve miles from Clayton, and the approach, by boat, is charming, as the pretty cottages come in view all along the shore, succeeded by the imposing hotel fronts as the harbor is neared. Among the handsome villas, that of the late Dr. J. G. Holland. "Bonnie Castle," is a conspicuous object, occupying a promontory which projects just below the landing.

THE THOUSAND ISLAND HOUSE,

A view of which we herewith present, is one of the finest hotels, both in point of its general arrangements and the natural advantages afforded by its location, to be found at any pleasure resort on the river. It is built on the solid rock, near the steamboat landing, and its windows command an extensive prospect, both up and down the river and across the Bay to Westminster Park. The view is still further expanded by ascending the lofty tower which adorns the center of the structure, rising 160 feet above the foundation, and surmounted with a balcony, affording an outlook of surpassing loveliness and grandeur. The hotel is the largest on the river, and will accommodate 700 guests.

THOUSAND ISLAND HOUSE, ALEXANDRIA BAY.

Leaving Alexandria Bay, we are now in the midst of the most fashionable part of the Thousand Island group. The residences are elegant in style of architecture and general appointments, some of them being very costly, their wealthy proprietors having lavished expenditure upon them with unstinted hand. The captain will call many of them by name, the islands having received their titles mostly from their present owners and occupants, and are somewhat fanciful and often appropriate. For instance "Fairy Land" seems a fitting abode for elfin sprites, although equally attractive to humanity. Arcadia, Sport Island, Summerland, Manhattan, Imperial, Welcome, Cozy, Nobby, and a host of other cognomens, have been bestowed upon the charming spots where taste, elegance, and refinement are exhibited, as art has united with nature in making them veritable summer paradises, where, let us hope, no serpent's trail may mar the happiness of their possessors.

The last of the Thousand Islands are called the Three Sisters, from their resemblance and proximity to each other. They are nearly opposite Brockville on the Canada shore and Morristown on the New York side, the two towns being directly opposite each other, the former the terminus of the Canadian Pacific Railway, and the latter of the Utica & Black River Railroad, needing only a bridge, with these islands as resting places for the abutments, to unite the two roads in one continuous line. Brockville, named in honor of General Brock, is called the "Queen City of the St. Lawrence," and there is something regal in its appearance to warrant the bestowment of the title. Its glittering towers and church spires give an appearance of splendor, which the tourist will observe as a peculiarity of the Canadian cities to be seen in his trip, the metal with which they are covered retaining its brightness in a remarkable degree, owing to the purity and dryness of the atmosphere.

OGDENSBURG AND PRESCOTT.

These two cities, like those last mentioned, are opposite each other, and are both important points. Ogdensburg is the terminus of the Rome, Watertown & Ogdensburg, the Utica & Black River, and Ogdensburg & Lake Champlain Railroads, the two former coming from the West and the latter from the East. The city lies on both sides of the Oswegatchie River, at its junction with the St. Lawrence. On account of its beautiful foliage, it has been appropriately entitled Maple City. Its extensive river front, with its railroad facilities, gives it a decided advantage as a grain port. Large elevators and warehouses for the transhipment of grain and other freight from the lake steamers are among the important enterprises of the place.

The direct route to the Adirondacks from Ogdensburg is *via* the Ogdensburg & Lake Champlain Railroad, on the line of which is also located the recently discovered but already famous Chateaugay Chasm. As the western section of the all-rail line from Ogdensburg to Portland, this railroad is also assuming considerable importance as a tourist route to the White Mountains and other resorts, and will receive due notice in a separate chapter.

Prescott, on the opposite bank of the St. Lawrence, is connected with Ogdensburg by ferry, the boats being of sufficient capacity to transfer cars, and making regular trips. The railroad interests of this place are concentrated in the Grand Trunk and the St. Lawrence & Ottawa division of the Canadian Pacific.

Massena Landing, where passengers destined for Massena Springs go ashore, is soon passed, and now a perceptible increase is noticeable in the velocity of the current. The interest among the passengers, if it has anywhere been allowed to flag, now becomes re-awakened, as the word goes along the line that the famous

RAPIDS OF THE ST. LAWRENCE

Will soon add zest to the journey. There are several courses of these rapids, those we are now entering being the Gallopes, which, compared with some of the others, are of but little interest, except as a foretaste of what is to come. Next we enter and pass the Rapid de Plau, and the excitement deepens as the foaming, seething waters just ahead proclaim the approach to the famous Long Sault (pronounced *Soo*). This is the longest of the series, being a continuous descent for nine miles, with the current running at a speed of twenty miles an hour. A canal, eleven miles in length, extends around this rapid, with seven locks, facilitating the descent of such crafts as are unable to cope with the rapids, and also permitting the return of the steamers. Four similar canals are to be met at various places along the river.

RUNNING THE RAPIDS.

"DOWN" VS. "UP"—RAPIDS AND CANAL.

At Dickenson's Landing, just before entering the Long Sault, the passengers are transferred to the "Prince Arthur," a boat constructed expressly for "shooting the rapids," which steams out from the landing, with its bow headed toward the angry waters, as if in defiance of their power. The increasing speed, and especially the perceptible descent, soon awaken the interest of the dullest among the passengers, and as the boat lurches to the right or left (or, in nautical phrase, to the starboard, or port), to escape destruction from some ledge which the trusty pilot knows how to avoid, the excitement deepens and increases, and the half hour required for the passage of the Long Sault is crowded full of alternating delight, fear and exhilaration, quickening the pulse and giving zest to the journey, not to be appreciated except by those who experience it.

At the foot of this Rapid, the placid waters of Lake St. Francis are entered, and the contrast between the tranquil surroundings and the tumult and excitement just passed through brings a grateful sense of relief, and the lovely scenery among which the boat now glides for twenty-five miles, is all the more keenly appreciated. The call to dinner, which is served during the passage of this lake, is a welcome one, and the passengers are now ready to descend to the level of things material and substantial, which they find spread in abundance in the dining saloon.

After dinner, and a quiet stroll on deck, a little more experience with rapids is in order. Passing Coteau du Lac, we enter the Coteau Rapids, descending quickly to the Cedars, Split Rock and Cascade Rapids. In passing the Cedars, a peculiar sensation is experienced, as the boat appears to settle down occasionally with great suddenness, as though about to be submerged. This is supposed to be owing to a strong undercurrent which exerts this influence on the boat as she passes from one ledge of rock to another, although they are at a safe distance below her keel. The passage of the Split Rock Rapids seems dangerous, as indeed it would be were the pilot to forget for a moment the grave responsibility of his trust, and fail to swerve the boat at just the right moment to avoid some rock or ledge that threatens destruction to the craft.

Occasionally a raft may be seen in conflict with the rushing waters, apparently at the mercy of the current. The venturesome lumbermen generally manage, however, to "put in an oar" to good advantage in steering clear of the rocks, although not always successful in guiding their frail crafts into quiet waters. An occasional wreck is the result of these ventures, as the scattering logs in the channel attest.

The Cascades are so called from their resemblance to a series of short, leaping falls. Passing the Cascades, we enter upon another broad expanse of water, the river here widening into Lake St. Louis, receiving also the waters of the Ottawa River. This lake is twelve miles long by about six in breadth, and the ride across its quiet waters just precedes the culminating excitement of the trip,—the daring passage of the

FAMOUS LACHINE RAPIDS.

At the head of these Rapids is the pretty little Indian village of Lachine, and here comes aboard our Indian pilot, Baptiste by name, who has piloted the boats through the Lachine Rapids for forty years. These Rapids are the most perilous in all the river's extent, on account of the devious nature of the channel, and the dangerous rocks which lie just enough below the surface to deceive any but the skillful navigator. The swarthy giant who takes the wheel at this point pays little attention to anything but the duty in hand, and that seems to demand all his energies. Casting alternate glances at him and at the rushing waters ahead of us, we involuntarily breathe the words of the hymn,

"Steady, O pilot, stand firm at the wheel."

RAFTS IN THE RAPIDS.

Right in our path lies a ragged rock, which threatens us with instant destruction; but a turn of the wheel at just the right moment sends our good craft a little to the left of it, and the apparent danger is past. With bated breath we watch for the next peril that looms ahead of us, to find it, like its predecessor, vanquished by the strong arm and steady nerve of the man to whom every inch of the channel is as familiar as a beaten path.

Entering once more into quiet waters, we steam on our way toward Montreal, and soon the horizon is marked with the long line of the famous VICTORIA BRIDGE, which rises higher and higher as we approach it, until we glide under it and are soon at the wharf of the American Line, at the close of a day that has been filled with a succession of delights unapproachable in a day's experience in travel elsewhere on the American Continent.

CANADIAN CARRYALL.

MONTREAL

— AND —

QUEBEC.

MONTREAL AND QUEBEC.

tour from the West to the East which did not include a visit to the chief cities of Canada would be indeed incomplete. Hence, in the arrangement of summer excursions, the River St. Lawrence comprising a part of the trip, it is both easy and natural to embrace these points of interest.

MONTREAL is the metropolis of British North America. Its situation, both from a scenic and commercial point of view, renders it attractive to the tourist and prosperous as a business center. Its location is on an island in the St. Lawrence, at the base of Mt. Royal, which gives the city its name. The view of the city from the river, with the mountain in the background is beautiful and impressive, and when this is supplemented by the grand picture exhibited from the summit of the mountain, with the river and the Victoria Bridge in the distance, the observer is ready to exclaim, "Beautiful for situation!"

On arriving in Montreal, whether by boat or rail, the traveler is impressed with the idea that the entire population must indulge in riding, so numerous are the hackmen, or carters, as they are called, to be seen at every hotel, depot and landing. Their easy one or two-horse carriages are at your service for long or short trips, and their prices are very reasonable, being regulated by law. The fare from point to point within the city is twenty-five cents for one or two passengers, and fifty cents for three or four, although the usual custom of the driver is to charge twenty-five cents for each passenger, and collect it if he can. If you go outside the city limits, make a bargain in advance. In fact, there is safety in giving this rule a general application wherever you need the services of a hackman, and thereby always avoiding contention in settlement.

CITY OF MONTREAL, FROM THE RIVER.

THE HOTELS

Of Montreal are excellent, comprising, among the most elegant, the Ottawa, Windsor, and St. Lawrence Hall. The Albion Hotel has for many years been a great favorite with American tourists, both from the *personnel* of its management and the reasonableness of its charges. The Montreal House, the American, the Richelieu, and a host of other claimants for patronage, all have their special merits, and are well-spoken of by their visitors.

Sight-seeing, in the city and vicinity, is best accomplished by the employment of a "carter," who is usually well posted on all the points of interest, and can often entertain his party with sundry legends in connection with them. The most delightful drive, for a single trip, is the

RIDE AROUND MOUNT ROYAL,

Which is about nine miles in extent, over splendid macadamized roads, through a section of country, in the suburbs, devoted to gardening, and under a high state of cultivation. The entire island, about thirty miles long by ten wide, is noted for its fertility, and is called the Garden of Canada. The trip should also include a drive to the summit of the mountain, which is reached by a carriage road of easy ascent, and which is being converted into a magnificent park, from which an extensive view of the city and surrounding country can be obtained. The Mount Royal Cemetery, the Grey Nunnery, and the Hotel Dieu are also to be seen in this drive, the latter being the largest building in the Dominion, used for a convent, hospital, and asylum for poor children.

The Water Works, the reservoir of which is on the side of the mountain, with the pumping station on the banks of the St. Lawrence, above the city, are well worthy of a visit. The reservoir was excavated out of the solid rock, and is 206 feet above the level of the river. The cost of the works, with the machinery, was over $2,000,000. The immense pressure obtained from such an elevated reservoir, enables the fire department to dispense entirely with engines, using hose carriages, and a large conflagration in the city is almost an impossibility.

The public buildings of the city are substantial and elegant, many of them conspicuous for their superior architectural design, and the completeness of their appointments. The Court House, Post Office, Merchants' Exchange, several bank buildings, the Custom House, McGill College, Bonsecours Market, and a list that might be indefinitely extended, comprise the notable structures that will attract attention as you ride through the business thoroughfares of the city.

The churches are among the finest to be found in America. Notre Dame, with its twin towers, conspicuous from every point of view, is the most capacious of any of the finished structures, although the Cathedral, now in process of erection, and modeled after St. Peter's at Rome, is to be second only to this famous edifice in point of size and elegance. The towers are massive and lofty, being 220 feet in height. The right-hand tower may be ascended, and the view to be had well rewards the effort of climbing. It contains the big bell, weighing nearly 30,000 pounds. The other tower contains a chime of bells. The Church of the Gesu is noted for the beauty of its frescoes and paintings. The English Cathedral, and several Protestant churches, are also fine edifices.

Lachine Canal, leading from above the rapids of that name, is a fine specimen of engineering, and not only serves to facilitate navigation, but furnishes almost unlimited water power for the extensive manufacturing enterprises along its banks.

MONTREAL, FROM MOUNT ROYAL PARK.

Victoria Bridge, which crosses the river from the Southern shore, is a massive and costly structure. One of the best views of it is that to be had in coming down the river, the boat passing under the central span. It is tubular in shape, built of iron, and rests upon twenty-four piers of solid masonry, the central span being 330 feet, and the remaining ones 242 feet. It cost $6,300,000, is the property of the Grand Trunk Railway Company, and is used exclusively for railway purposes.

The shipping interests of Montreal are among the most important sources of the city's prosperity. At the head of ocean navigation, it is the American terminus of a number of trans-Atlantic steamship lines, and the railway and river and lake connections from the West, combined with its facilities for ocean commerce, render it very prominent as a port for transhipment. Its wharves are not excelled in America, being constructed of solid limestone; and its harbor is deep and capacious.

The Champ de Mars, a spacious parade ground, where three thousand troops may be reviewed at once; Viger Square, near by, with gardens, conservatories, fountains, etc.; Victoria Square, Jacques Cartier Square, and several other smaller squares, constitute the parks of the city, in addition to the Mount Royal Park. Improve his time as he may, the visitor will not soon exhaust the attractions of this beautiful city, and will find many more, which we have not space even to mention, as we regretfully leave the pleasant spot, and resume our journey, to the

ANCIENT CITY OF QUEBEC.

The route from Montreal may be chosen from three: The North Shore Railway, the Grand Trunk Railway, and the Richelieu & Ontario Steamship Line *via* the St. Lawrence. The latter is a favorite, and unless the tourist is surfeited with steamboat riding, will be the one generally chosen. It is a night trip, and therefore less wearisome than a ride by rail, as the comfortable state rooms of the boat are preferable to the berths of a sleeping-car.

CITY OF QUEBEC, FROM THE RIVER.

Leaving Montreal at early evening, passing the fort on the island directly against the city, and onward past the mouth of the Ottawa River below the city, the first stop is at the town of Sorel, or William Henry, at the confluence of Sorel or Richelieu River, forty-five miles from Montreal. Five miles farther on, the river expands into a lake about twenty-five miles in length by nine in width, and known as Lake St. Peter. Next we come to the ancient city of Three Rivers, taking its name from the fact that the St. Maurice River, which here flows into the St. Lawrence, is divided by islands into three channels.

The view of Quebec, as approached from the river, is singularly impressive. Unlike any other city on the American continent, its situation and surroundings make it an object of striking interest. The fortifications, with their towers and battlements, frown upon you from the Plains of Abraham and from the lower town, and there surrounds the place an air of mediævalism at once novel and attractive.

It is one of the oldest cities in America, as well as one of the most interesting. It was founded in 1608, and its history is replete with events of tremendous importance. The scene of many a battle and of untold carnage, the crowning event of all was the memorable engagement which transferred half a continent from France to Britain, and immortalized the names of both commanders, the victor and the vanquished.

CITY AND HARBOR OF QUEBEC, FROM THE CITADEL.

The city consists of two divisions, known as the upper and the lower town.
The upper town includes within its limits the Citadel of Cape Diamond, which
covers the entire summit of the promontory, embracing an area of more than forty

acres. It rises to the height of 345 feet above the river, and from its commanding position and the strength of the fortification, has been not inaptly entitled the "Gibraltar of America."

CAPE DIAMOND.

The shape of the city is triangular, the St. Lawrence and St. Charles rivers forming the two sides, with the Plains of Abraham for the base. The river fronts are defended by a continuous wall on the very brow of the cliff, with flanking towers and bastions, loopholed for musketry and pierced for cannon. On the west side, a heavy triple wall, with trenches between, formerly guarded that approach, but much of it is now demolished. Between the old town and the outside world, the wall was formerly pierced with frowning gateways, five in number; but these have been gradually demolished, in response to the increasing demand for more free communication, and on the occasion of the writer's last visit to the city, the old Saint John's gate was being entirely removed. We present views of these gateways, from which the fortified aspect of the town before their demolition may be readily inferred.

The nationality of the inhabitants is strongly French, and the visitor from the States can easily fancy himself in a city in France, so decidedly un-American are all his surroundings. The quaint houses, the steep and tortuous streets, especially of the oldest portions of the city, and the almost universal use of the French language in the ordinary channels of trade, require no stretch of the imagination to practically transport one to the old world, and give a glimpse, as it were, of a foreign country.

WOLFE'S OLD MONUMENT.

The view from the Citadel, on account of its elevation, is surpassingly grand and comprehensive. The majestic St. Lawrence, alive with sailing craft of every size and kind, stretches before the vision in both directions, seeming like a band of glistening metal, beautifying the scene and giving animation to the picture. Directly below lie the crooked streets of the lower town, teeming with animation, while its busy population so far beneath, seem like pigmies, and you look upon the glistening roofs of the houses and down the very throats of the chimneys, into which it would seem an easy matter to toss a pebble.

WOLFE'S NEW MONUMENT.

Looking to the westward, the Plains of Abraham are spread out before you, together with the bluffs scaled by Wolfe and his brave soldiers in the preparation for the assault that ended in a victory, but cost the lives of both commanders. The spot where Wolfe fell is marked by a handsome monument. It was erected in 1849, but is still called the "new monument" in distinction from the simple monolith which previously occupied its site, an illustration of which is given on the preceding page. The new monument bears the simple but eloquent inscription, "Here died Wolfe, victorious." Directly across the river is the settlement of Point Levi, and down the stream the beautiful Isle of Orleans may be seen. This pleasant resort may be reached by ferry from the city, and it affords delightful drives, giving views of the Falls of Montmorenci, the Laurentian Mountains, and other objects of interest.

Chaudiere Falls, nine miles above Quebec, on the river of the same name, are 130 feet high and 400 feet wide. The Falls and Indian village of Lorette, seven miles from Quebec, are points to which excursions may be profitably made, either by carriage or the North Shore Railway.

Other points of interest in and about Quebec demand at least a brief mention. The Dufferin Terrace, which will be included in the visit to the Plains of Abraham, as will also the Governor's Garden, where the monument to Wolfe and Montcalm will be seen; the French Cathedral; the Laval Seminary, in the chapel of which are some very fine paintings; the English Cathedral, near by; the Ursuline Convent; the public buildings in the lower town, and others which the driver will point out to you, are of sufficient interest to enliven a visit of several days duration, or they may be hurriedly inspected in a "flying trip."

PALACE GATE, QUEBEC.

ST. LOUIS GATE, QUEBEC.

FRENCH CANADIAN HOME.

FALLS OF MONTMORENCI.

THE FALLS OF MONTMORENCI

Are among the most interesting of the objects which secure the visits of tourists to Quebec, both on account of their own attractiveness and the pleasant drive by which they are reached. The "carters" of Quebec are as numerous as those of Montreal, and the roads around the city and in the country adjacent are among the finest to be found anywhere. Securing your driver, you leave the city by one of the gates, and, crossing the St. Charles River, are soon in the suburbs, passing here and there a house or villa of modern style, but speedily coming to the realm of the ancient; the road leading through quaint old hamlets, the cottages with their picturesque dormer windows, the thatched-roofed outbuildings, and the peasant-like appearance of the people, combined with the universal employment of the French language, strengthen the fancy for the time being that America must be far away, and that the rural districts of France or Switzerland are the scenes through which your trip is made. Children run beside the carriage, asking alms or offering flowers, while the women and older girls are at work in the fields, or spinning with their rude wheels in the open doorways or on the porches of the little houses. The antiquated implements of agriculture, the rude carts by the roadside, and the rustic crosses by the way, at which some devout pilgrim, perchance, is tarrying to breathe a *Pater Noster*, all tend to complete the illusion of a remoter age or more distant clime than the few hours' ride from bustling, modern, Yankee civilization.

The ride of eight miles all too quickly brings you to the River Montmorenci, and here you gaze upon historic ground, it being the scene of the battle of Montmorenci which immediately preceded Wolfe's final victory at Quebec. Leaving your carriage, and paying a small fee for the privilege of crossing private grounds, you descend the bank of the river to look up at the fall from below. The river here pours over the cliff into the St. Lawrence, broadening at the edge to about 50 feet, and falling 250, in a sheeny vail, half water, half spray, not sublime, nor even grand, but exquisitely beautiful.

The towers on either side of the river still mark the spot where, several years ago, a suspension bridge was erected, but which, through some defect, gave way as a laborer and his family were crossing in a cart, precipitating them into the gulf below.

Returning to Quebec, the views of the city are enlivened by the peculiar feature of glistening towers and roofs, so noticeable in connection with many Canadian cities. The sunlight, glancing from the metal-covered roofs, spires, and dormer windows, which, owing to the tortuous windings of the streets, are set at every conceivable angle, produces a brilliant and sparkling effect.

If you are ever tempted to indulge in sentiment, the words of the poet, used to describe the Celestial city, may come into mind: —

> "There is the city in splendor sublime;
> See how its towers and battlements shine."

THE SAGUENAY RIVER.

This is the largest affluent of the St. Lawrence, which it joins about 120 miles below Quebec. The scenery of the Saguenay is strikingly grand and romantic, and unlike anything else east of the Rocky Mountains. It is usually visited by boat, and the trip down the St. Lawrence to Tadousac, at the junction of the two streams, and up the Saguenay among its bold, wild scenery, should not be omitted, even at the expense of slighting some other point of interest lying in the highways of fashionable travel.

Leaving Quebec by steamer, you pass through some remarkably fine scenery, in which the majestic St. Lawrence abounds, the river being in some places thirty miles in width, and dotted with a multitude of islands, abounding in game. The Falls of St. Anne are on the river of that name, which enters the St. Lawrence off the lower end of Orleans Island through a bold ravine. The quarantine station on Grosse Isle is passed, and is associated with sad memories of the famine in Ireland. It received twenty thousand plague-stricken emigrants, of whom six thousand now lie in a single grave, marked by a stone monument.

Ninety miles below Quebec is the fashionable watering place known as Murray Bay. The river is here twenty miles wide, and the tides have a range of twenty feet in height. On the south shore of the river, still further down, is Riviere du Loup, a place of some importance, and six miles below it is Cacouna, already quite famous as a pleasure resort, and yearly increasing in popularity. Across the river from Cacouna is Tadousac, at the mouth of the far-famed Saguenay, formerly a place of some commercial importance as a post of the Hudson Bay Company, and one of the first towns on the St. Lawrence fortified by the French. It has a good hotel, near which is a little church over 250 years old.

TADOUSAC, AT MOUTH OF SAGUENAY RIVER.

The Saguenay River is remarkable, not only for its great depth, but also for the marvelous height of its banks. It seems to flow through a rift in the Laurentian Mountains, which appear to be cleft, as it were, to the very foundations, the height of the cliffs rising from the edge of the river being equaled only by the depth to which they descend below the surface. The source of the river is 130 miles from its junction with the St. Lawrence, in Lake St. John, which is fed by eleven rivers, draining an immense watershed, the great volume resultant pouring through this remarkable gorge, in many places unfathomable. At St. John's Bay, 27 miles above Tadousac, the water is one mile and a half in depth, and but little less at Eternity Bay, six miles beyond. At the latter place, the wonderful capes, Trinity and Eternity, like giant sentinels guard the entrance, rising 1,500 and 1,900 feet, respectively, above the water.

Ha-Ha Bay is sixty miles above Tadousac, and is nine miles long by six wide. It has also been named Grand Bay. The first-named title is said to have come from the exclamations of delight which sprung from the lips of the navigators of the river on its discovery; and in contrast with the gloomy and forbidding aspect of the lower portions of the river, it would seem that such an outburst might be perfectly natural. The mountains around Ha-Ha Bay abound in whortleberries, or blueberries, as they are here called, and a very important industry with the natives is the gathering and shipment to market of the bountiful harvest thus kindly furnished by nature, the picking season extending from the middle of July until the falling of the snow, and the supply being inexhaustible.

HA-HA BAY, SAGUENAY RIVER.

Chicoutimi, a few miles beyond, is at the head of navigation, the river being obstructed above this point by rapids and falls. Lumbering is one of its important industries, the immense forests of the vicinity being as yet almost in their virgin state, and the harbor accessible to the largest vessels, thus giving it natural facilities of great value.

CAPES ETERNITY AND TRINITY.

INDIAN CURIOSITY SELLER.

The fishing in the Saguenay River and its tributaries is one of the chief attractions to the sportsman. Salmon abound, and the quality of the fish taken from such deep, cold water can readily be inferred by the disciples of Walton. Game also abounds in the forests, some specimens being well worthy of the skill and nerve of the trained hunter.

A student of character will find an interesting subject in the person of the Canadian Indian, to be met in various localities in Canada. Combining with his native craft the shrewdness of a Connecticut Yankee, he will often appear in the role of a vender of curiosities, in which "taking" attitude our artist presents him.

In closing our notes on the Saguenay, we feel that but faint justice can be done to its wonderful attractions. It has been tersely described by a writer as a "region of primeval grandeur, where art has done nothing and nature everything; where, at a single bound, civilization is left behind and nature stands in unadorned majesty; where Alps on Alps arise; where, over unfathomable depths, through mountain gorges, the steamer ploughs the dark flood on which no sign of animal life appears." A better summing up of its peculiar features, in so few words, could not be written, and the tourist who visits the scenes we have briefly described will indulge in no regrets, unless it be that want of time to do justice to the trip gives only hurried glances where hours and days might be enjoyed in realizing the sublime grandeur of the surroundings.

OGDENSBURG TO PORTLAND.

he route by the "all-rail" line from the St. Lawrence at Ogdensburg to the ocean at Portland, presents many attractions to the pleasure tourist, which we deem worthy of special mention in this connection. As an avenue of approach to the Adirondacks, Chateaugay Chasm, the Green Mountains of Vermont, and the White Mountains of New Hampshire, it offers a combination of desirable routes for summer travel. Indeed, the entire line extends through a succession of lake, river, and mountain scenery, of charming beauty and variety.

THE ADIRONDACKS are best reached by way of MALONE, a station on the Ogdensburg & Lake Champlain Railroad, about sixty miles from Ogdensburg. From here an excellent stage line takes the tourist to the Adirondack Wilderness, by way of Ayer's, Loon Lake, Meacham Lake, and St. Regis, the latter being the location of "Paul Smith's" famous hostelry. CHATEAUGAY, a station twelve miles east of Malone, is another gateway to the famous resort, the stages going *via* the Chateaugay Lakes.

The "Adirondack District" is a term applied to a tract of country having for its general boundaries the St. Lawrence River on the north, Lakes Champlain and George on the east, the Mohawk River on the south, and the Black River on the west. The encroachments of civilization have so trenched upon these boundaries, that the "Wilderness," so called, comprises only the central, unsettled and uncultivated portion of this tract, almost in its primeval state, with a border of settled country on all sides. The limits of this work forbid an extended description of this region, which as yet is only partially explored. Indeed, one of its chief delights consists in the new discoveries that the venturesome tourist may make in his search for the game which abounds in its forests, or the fish which teem in its waters.

The following, from the report of the Superintendent of the Adirondack Survey, gives a good idea of the character of some portions of this wilderness:—

"In these remote sections, tilled with rugged mountains, where unnamed waterfalls pour in snowy tresses from the dark, overhanging cliffs, the horse can find no footing, and the adventurous trapper or explorer must carry upon his back his blankets and a heavy stock of food. His rifle, which affords protection against wild beasts, at times replenishes his well-husbanded provisions, and his axe aids him in constructing from bark or bough, some temporary shelter from storm, or hews into logs the huge trees which form the fierce, roaring, comfortable fire of the camp. Yet, though the woodman may pass his lifetime in some section of the wilderness, it is still a mystery to him. ** It is a peculiar region; for though the geographical center of the wilderness may be readily and easily reached in the light, canoe-like boats of the guides, by lakes and rivers, which form a labyrinth of passages for boats, the core, or rather cores of this wilderness extend on either hand from these broad avenues of water, and, in their interior, spots remain to-day as untrodden by man, and as unknown and wild, as when the Indian paddled his birchen boat upon those streams and lakes. Amid these mountain solitudes are places where, in all probability, the foot of man never trod; and here the panther has his den among the rocks, and rears his savage kittens undisturbed, save by the growl of bear or screech of lynx, or the hoarse croak of raven taking its share of the carcass of slain deer."

CASCADE AND BUTTRESS.

GIANT GORGE—PULPIT ROCK.

A mile and a half north of Chateaugay is the wonderful CHATEAUGAY CHASM, a newly discovered rival of the far-famed Ausable. The waters of the Chateaugay Lakes here find a passage on their way to the St. Lawrence, through a narrow gorge, walled in by sandstone cliffs, the river in one place making a descent of fifty feet in a beautiful cascade. Several of the more noticeable features of this wonderful chasm are presented in our illustrations. The "Cascade and Buttress" exhibits an appearance of constructive design, as layer upon layer of sandstone rock forms a terraced buttress, resembling some ancient ruin. "Giant Gorge" is a narrow defile, with frowning walls, having the romantic and interesting feature of a cavern, called "Vulcan's Cave," with an entrance in the side of the rock, sixty feet above the river, and one hundred and twenty feet below the top of the cliff. It was first explored by means of spliced ladders, but is now reached by an enclosed stairway. It is about thirty feet square, and presents an interesting study for the geologist. The cave was doubtless hollowed out of the sandstone by the action of water which trickled down through the ledge above in tiny streams, wearing away the softer stone by slow degrees, and leaving the masses of harder deposit in a variety of singular and grotesque shapes. A series of architectural pillars, supporting gothic arches or miniature dormer windows, may be seen on the one hand, and at certain angles, odd and fantastic figures, some of them half human in appearance, present themselves, while here and there a block of stone appears like the unfinished work of the sculptor.

SPARTAN PASS—RAINBOW FALLS.

PIONEER CROSSING—POINT LOOKOUT.

"Spartan Pass" and "Rainbow Basin and Falls" are peculiarly interesting, the water descending to the basin over a succession of rocky steps, nearly a hundred in number, coming to a rest in the "basin," only to dash on again, in ever-changing forms and merry cadence, in their race through the gorge, to the St. Lawrence. "Pioneer Crossing" receives its name from the fact that in early times a bridge spanned the chasm, on what was then the great highway of the wilderness. On the north side of this crossing a huge rock affords an extensive view of the gorge, from which fact it has been named Point Lookout. In other parts of the Chasm, grottoes, arches, columns, etc., afford subjects of study for the curious, and of admiration for the lovers of the odd and fantastic in nature. A fine hotel has been erected near the entrance to the chasm, from the cupola of which splendid views may be had of the scenery. Coaches connect with trains at Chateaugay.

At Rouse's Point, the terminus of the O. & L. C. R. R., connection is made with the Delaware & Hudson Canal Co. Railroad for Lake George, Saratoga, Troy, Albany, and New York, and with the Central Vermont for St. Albans, Worcester, Providence and Boston. Continuing our journey toward Portland, we here traverse a small portion of the Central Vermont Railroad to Swanton, where connection is made with the

ST. JOHNSBURY & LAKE CHAMPLAIN RAILROAD,

The next link in the line under consideration. The route from Rouse's Point, *via* Lake Champlain, is exceedingly pleasant, the scenery being that of the lovely lake, and the Green Mountains of Vermont. SHELDON SPRINGS are on the line of this road, and it is also a direct route to MOUNT MANSFIELD. Both these localities have acquired no little celebrity as summer resorts.

At Morrisville, connection is made for Mount Mansfield by stage line, and such as wish to visit the locality will find an excellent stopping place at Mt. Mansfield House. The mountain is in the town of Stowe, about twenty miles northeast of Montpelier, and its height is 4,359 feet above the level of the sea.

The Green Mountains of Vermont are a portion of the great Appalachian range, extending almost continuously from near the St. Lawrence River, in Canada, through the entire length of Vermont, across the western part of Massachusetts and the middle Atlantic States, to the northern part of Alabama. The White Mountains of New Hampshire, and the Adirondacks and Catskills of New York are regarded as outlying spurs of this chain. This range is remarkable for the uniformity of outline which characterizes the different peaks, particularly of their summits, the ridges extending in the same general direction, sometimes hardly diverging from a straight line for a distance of fifty or sixty miles. Where the mountain chains are parallel, the ridges are also in parallel lines, preserving their general direction, and, to a wonderful extent, a uniformity of distance between them. When one curves round in a new direction, all curve with it.

These general peculiarities are less marked in the mountains of Vermont than in the more southerly portions of the same chain. In fact, the peculiar characteristics of the range, as a whole, are less marked at both its northern and southern extremities, the termination at either end not being well defined, as the mountains sink away and are lost in the hilly country that succeeds to them.

The Green Mountain peaks are also less bold and abrupt than those of the White Mountains, being covered mostly with verdure to their very summits, and presenting less of sharp or ragged outline in their general conformation. To many visitors, this feature is pleasing and agreeable, and a large class of summer tourists spend a portion or all of the season in the vicinity of the "beautiful hills" of the "Green Mountain State."

At St. Johnsbury the line intersects the Passumpsic Railroad, and a description of the route from this point will be given in the following chapter, in connection with the trip from Quebec and Montreal.

The White Mountains.

THE WHITE MOUNTAINS.

The route from the West to the seaboard *via* Montreal and Quebec, as arranged over recently completed lines of travel, naturally extends through the charming region of the celebrated White Hills of New Hampshire. From Montreal, or any point beyond, this popular resort is easy of access by several routes, all of them possessing some special attraction to invite the tourist to give them a trial. From Quebec, the tourist may return to Montreal, by boat or rail, or may proceed directly to the mountains by the QUEBEC CENTRAL RAILWAY to Sherbrooke, thence *via* the Passumpsic Railroad to St. Johnsbury, Bethlehem and Fabyans, in the very heart of the White Mountain region.

If the trip be made by way of Montreal, the mountains may be reached *via* the Grand Trunk, the Southeastern, or the Central Vermont. The route by the Grand Trunk, is by way of Gorham, and the eastern side of the mountains. By the Southeastern, the line is to Newport and St. Johnsbury. The Central Vermont line offers two routes; one to Montpelier, there connecting with the Montpelier & Wells River Railroad, or by way of Swanton, thence by the Portland and Ogdensburg line to St. Johnsbury, which thus seems to be made the focus of all the various lines having the same general direction, and leading to the mountain region.

At NEWPORT, reached by the Southeastern from Montreal, or the Quebec Central from Quebec, the celebrated Lake Memphremagog is the chief attraction, and the dining station is at the splendid hotel bearing the same name as the lake. It is a popular summer resort, and the steamer on the lake makes frequent trips for the accommodation of tourists. Several mountains, comprising Jay Peak, Owl's Head, Mount Oxford, Mount Elephantis and the Willoughby Mountains are among the attractions of the vicinity.

WHITE MOUNTAIN RANGE.

St. Johnsbury is situated on the Passumpsic River, at the intersection of the Passumpsic and St. Johnsbury & Lake Champlain Railroads; and in addition to the attractiveness of its location from a scenic point of view, it has attained much prominence as a manufacturing town, the heaviest enterprise in that direction being the production of the celebrated Fairbanks scales, known the world over for their excellence and correctness. The St. Johnsbury House and Avenue Hotel are good places of entertainment.

Eastward from St. Johnsbury the route lies over the St. Johnsbury & Lake Champlain Railroad to Lunenburg, the western terminus of the Portland division of the P. & O. line. From this point, a ride of an hour brings us into the very midst of the glorious White Hills, and in full view of the grand

PRESIDENTIAL RANGE,

Stretching before the vision in a glorious and beautiful panorama, with the peerless WASHINGTON above them all. This approach to the mountains affords the most comprehensive view of the principal range; and the Westerner, who has always been accustomed to broad expanses of prairie, with no greater elevations, perhaps, than the height of an ordinary church steeple, will be peculiarly impressed with the grandeur of the scene before him.

The first important station is BETHLEHEM JUNCTION, three miles from Bethlehem village, the "paradise of hay-fever sufferers." This lovely hamlet enjoys the distinction of having the highest location of any town in the United States east of the Rockies and north of the Carolinas; and the remarkable purity of its atmosphere not only secures exemption from the peculiar malady which drives so many to its protection, but heightens the effect of the views to be had of the surrounding country. Owing to its commanding position, and the remarkable clearness of the atmosphere, the view of the mountains from "Bethlehem Street" is confessedly the best to be had anywhere.

The village is rendered accessible to the traveler by means of a recently constructed narrow-gauge railroad, from Bethlehem Junction to the end of the "street." About midway on the line of this road is the magnificent hotel known as MAPLE-WOOD, kept in superb style, and at its terminus is the well-known SINCLAIR HOUSE, Durgin & Fox proprietors. In addition to these palace hotels, a host of smaller ones, and a long list of boarding-houses, furnish abiding places for the multitudes who "tarry for a night," or make this place their summer home.

Bethlehem is also the railroad connection for the famous FRANCONIA NOTCH, by means of a narrow-gauge railroad, extending into the valley and terminating near the Profile House. The attractions of this locality are sufficiently important to demand special notice by themselves; and we therefore keep straight on in our course, the next stop being at the TWIN MOUNTAIN HOUSE, so named from its proximity to the "Twin Mountains," one of which is visible from the hotel. This house has for many years been the summer home of Henry Ward Beecher, who addresses large congregations of Sunday excursionists during the season.

Four miles further, and we stop at the WHITE MOUNTAIN HOUSE, one of the oldest of the mountain hotels, a veritable "tavern" of the earlier days, with less of style than its more pretentious neighbors, but with a large stock of good cheer and hospitable care for its guests, at moderate prices. Only a mile from the Fabyan House, the would-be guests of the latter are sometimes compelled, from an over-taxation of its immense capacities, to fall back on the resources of mine host Rounsevel, who gives them the best his house affords, and bids them "be therewith content."

SINCLAIR HOUSE, BETHLEHEM.

THE FABYAN HOUSE,

Six miles from the base of Mount Washington, is one of the most complete establishments of its kind in all the mountain region, having accommodations for five hundred guests. It is situated on a beautiful intervale, at an elevation of more than fifteen hundred feet above sea level, and its piazzas afford a fine view of the White Mountain range. It is also a central point from which excursions are made to the various resorts within easy reach by rail or carriage. The traveler may find, in this vicinity, an opportunity to enjoy a relic of the "good old days" of stage-coaching, which the railway has not succeeded in entirely abolishing, although it has largely superseded the conveyance once so popular in the mountain region.

FABYAN HOUSE, WHITE MOUNTAINS.

THE ASCENT OF MOUNT WASHINGTON.

From the Fabyan House, the railroad has been extended to the base of Mount Washington, there connecting with the wonderful elevated railway to the summit, thus forming a continuous all-rail line to the realm above the clouds. The six miles of road to the base of the mountain compasses some of the steepest grades known to railroad engineering. A powerful engine, of the six-drive-wheel construction, is required to propel a very moderate load of passengers, and as it laboriously puffs along the grades, the forests echo and re-echo with the sound, while the traveler feels thankful that the iron horse, instead of flesh and blood, is being employed in his service.

Mt. Pleasant Hotel is passed a short distance from Fabyan's, and a short distance from here are the WILD AMMONOOSUC FALLS, a natural curiosity well worthy of a visit. The river descends "about fifty feet, in a broken, irregular way, and in some places has worn curious channels in the rocks, resembling a cauldron, in which the water seethes and boils in its downward course, and issues laughing, singing and leaping in its wild and merry race for the intervales below."

THE MOUNT WASHINGTON RAILWAY is one of the wonders of modern engineering skill. It was chartered by the Legislature of New Hampshire, in 1858, the passage of the bill being regarded as the huge joke of the session, one member offering to amend it by "extending it to the moon," either terminal being regarded as equally liable to become a fact. In spite of obstacles, however, its construction was successfully accomplished, by the combined ingenuity of the projector and inventor, Sylvester Marsh, the mechanical skill of Walter Aiken, who built the engine and cars, and the financial aid and "push" of friendly individuals and interested railway companies. It was completed in 1869, and has carried thousands up and down the mountain without the slightest injury to any, so complete is the system of safety appliances in use, each independent of the other, and any one sufficient in itself to insure complete safety. The writer was once an eye-witness to the severest test to which it has ever yet been subjected, caused by the breakage of one of the gear driving wheels of the locomotive. The resultant disarrangement of the machinery set in operation the automatic safeguards, producing the effect of instantly holding the train to the track as firmly as though it had been bolted to the solid rock. Indeed, it was with no little difficulty that it was liberated, and enabled to proceed.

The accompanying illustration gives a good idea of the operation of the road. In addition to the ordinary rails of the common railroad, there is a toothed rail midway between, in which there "meshes" the geared wheel attached to the axle of the locomotive, which thus steadily *climbs* up the mountain by the revolution of the machinery. All the axles, both of the engine and passenger coach, are provided with geared wheels, by means of which the train could be instantly anchored to the track, as in the case above cited. Each car has its own locomotive, and will carry about fifty passengers. The seats are inclined backward, so as to be in a good position on ascending the mountain. The car is always above the engine, both in the ascent and descent. The latter is accomplished by gravitation alone, the brakes being kept in requisition to hold the train in check.

MT. WASHINGTON RAILWAY.

The ride up the mountain constitutes an experience never to be forgotten. Leaving Ammonoosuc Station, as the starting point at the base is called, the train immediately surmounts a considerable elevation before emerging from the forest, which is soon left behind as we rise above the "tree-line," and reach the region of stunted shrubs, which in turn give place to moss and lichens, and finally to rocks, bare of vegetation, and as cheerless as it is possible to imagine. Above the trees, the prospect broadens, as the landscape spreads out in a grand panorama, almost illimitable, and of wonderful grandeur and beauty. Several stops are made for water, which is taken from large tanks fed by mountain springs, far above, and conducted down in pipes. These stopping places have been appropriately named, according to their location, such as Waumbek Station, Gulf Station, etc., the latter being near the yawning chasm in the mountain-side, named the GULF OF MEXICO. Banks of snow may frequently be seen in its recesses, even in midsummer, and a game of snowballing is not an uncommon August recreation.

JACOB'S LADDER is a long section of trestle work, with a considerable elevation and steep inclination, after passing which the grade diminishes somewhat, as the road winds around the crown of the mountain.

Near the summit is a pile of rocks surmounted by a tablet, known as the "Lizzie Bourne Monument," marking the spot where the young lady perished from exposure, in September, 1855; having undertaken the ascent of the mountain in company with two male relatives, without a guide, and becoming chilled and bewildered, she lost her way, and despairingly sank down to die almost in sight of the summit.

"GULF OF MEXICO," MT. WASHINGTON.

Nearing the summit, the view changes, as the scenery of the eastern side comes in view. The highlands of Maine are now the background of the picture, with intervening valleys, lakes and rivers, while far below, the white buildings of the Glen House dot the landscape as a mere speck in the lovely valley in which they nestle.

The trip from base to summit occupies about an hour and a quarter, the distance being three miles, with an average grade of 1,300 feet to the mile, the most abrupt ascent being in the proportion of one foot in three. An approximate idea of this grade may be had by placing a yard-stick upon a level surface, as a table, and raising one end of it a foot, with the other end upon the table. Then imagine a train of cars climbing such an ascent, and you have a fair conception of the grade; but the most vivid imagination would fail to take in the sensations actually experienced in the journey.

LIZZIE BOURNE MONUMENT.

THE MOUNT WASHINGTON SUMMIT HOUSE.

The provisions for the entertainment of guests at the summit were formerly very limited, a few rude stone structures furnishing shelter for such as dared brave the hardships of a night in the clouds. But now all is changed. The capacious and comfortable building which serves the double purpose of depot and hotel, not only provides comfortable shelter, but a first-class table and excellent fare for about one hundred and fifty guests. The house was opened to the public in 1873, and has been in successful operation since, sometimes being taxed to its utmost capacity.

MOUNT WASHINGTON SUMMIT HOUSE.

The view from the summit is indescribably grand. At an altitude of 6,193 feet, or more than a mile and one-fifth above sea-level, the line of vision bounds a circle nearly a thousand miles in circumference; and within that circle are lakes, rivers, mountains, valleys, dark forests, smiling villages, and in fact a variety of scenery, ever changing as the gaze is directed to the different points of the compass. In a clear day, the distant glimmer of the Atlantic may be seen, away to the southeast. A little more to the south a brighter gleam reveals the location of Lake Winnipesaukee, while the Saco valley and Chocorua Mountain are in the nearer foreground. Turning still to the right, you see other mountains of the range on whose highest summit you are standing, Mount Monroe, the Twin Ponds, Mount Pleasant, Mount Franklin, Mount Willey, the scene of the famous "slide," and lesser elevations beyond.

MOUNTS ADAMS AND MADISON.

Westward, away in the dim distance, the horizon is broken by the Green Mountains of Vermont, with an occasional view of the remote Adirondacks in New York; while nearer, you see the valley of the Ammonoosuc, the Fabyan House, Bethlehem, Mount Lafayette, and the expanse of forest which fills the picture. To the northwest, the villages of Littleton, Jefferson and Lancaster appear, while in the distance, to the north, the table lands of Canada unite with the sky in bounding the horizon. To the northeast, the eye reaches to the unbroken forests of Maine. Mount Katahdin throws its dim outline against the sky, while in the foreground Mounts Jefferson, Adams and Madison tower grandly up before you as a grim body-guard to Washington. Nestled in the glen, the white hotel buildings of the Glen House establishment are visible; while near at hand, toward the southeast, Mount Jackson appears, and in the distance, the Pequaket or Kiarsarge may be seen, together with Sebago Lake in Maine.

WHITE MOUNTAINS, FROM JEFFERSON.

CLIMBING MOUNT JEFFERSON.

SUNRISE ON MOUNT WASHINGTON.

DISTANT VIEW OF MOUNT WASHINGTON.

The grand, culminating view from this lofty point of observation is to be had at the rising of the sun. For this incomparable prospect you must spend a night among the clouds, and perchance more than one night, as nature is fickle at that altitude as well as in the valleys below, and not unfrequently "old Sol" has half a forenoon's work before him to dispel "the mists of the morning" before his face is visible to the watchers on the summit. Should you be favored, however, with both a clear sunrise and sunset in one day, as was the writer on the occasion of his first visit, you will cherish in the chambers of memory the most enchanting pictures of a lifetime. Sunset at sea has awakened the lyre of many a poet, and inspired the pencil of many a painter; but neither pen nor pencil can give an adequate picture of the beauties of a sunrise as viewed from the summit of Mount Washington.

At early dawn the inmates of the house are roused, and such as choose arise and dress, and take their position on the platform east of the building, to watch for the first appearance of the "golden orb of day." Beneath you the valleys are still in slumber, and a deep gloom is spread over all, in sharp contrast with the light of dawn which already illumines the mountain peaks around you. Banks of mist here and there indicate the location of bodies of water, and possibly overhanging clouds may partially hide some of the mountain summits from view.

WATCHING FOR SUNRISE.

All eyes are turned expectantly towards the east, which is beginning to show a faint rosy tinge, deepening every moment till it reaches a crimson or perhaps a golden hue, a fitting couch from which the brilliant day king is about to spring forth to enter upon his glorious reign. Suddenly one point in the eastern horizon grows more intensely bright than all the rest, and the disc of the sun is then discernible, quickly increasing in proportions until the broad face of the great luminary so dazzles the eye as to compel a withdrawal of the gaze.

TIP-TOP HOUSE IN WINTER.

Looking then into the valleys below, the effect is transcendently beautiful. While the spectator is bathed in the full golden sunshine, the somber shadows are just beginning to flit away, presenting in the strongest possible manner the contrasts of light and shade; and not until some minutes have elapsed, does the new-born day reach down into the deepest valleys to drive forth the lingering remnants of night.

The view of the mountain peaks around, as, one after another, according to their height, they are touched by the rays of the rising sun, is very beautiful; and even the dullest mind can scarcely resist the enthusiastic inspiration awakened by the scene. And then, as the sun mounts steadily upward, giving heat as well as light with his cheering rays, the mists below are slowly dispelled, and nature puts on her most bewitching countenance, with her gloomy frowns banished, supplanted by the sweetest smiles.

Such is but a faint description of a sunrise witnessed by the writer. The picture will vary with the changing circumstances, and that which it may be the reader's fortune to behold, though entirely unlike it, may be none the less beautiful and enchanting.

MOUNT GARFIELD.

The old Tip-Top and Summit Houses still stand, together with the buildings of the U. S. Signal Service, the ticket-office and station of the Glen House stage line, with its stables, and the engine house of the railway. The office of *Among the Clouds*, a daily paper, occupies the old Tip-Top House; and in the Signal Service building a band of resolute men brave the rigors of winter in the interests of science, recording the temperature, the velocity of the wind, etc. With the thermometer at fifty degrees below zero, and the wind blowing with a velocity of one hundred and fifty miles an hour, it must require nerves of steel and a hardy constitution to survive the ordeal.

The old bridle path from the Crawford House to the summit is still employed by those who wish to make the ascent, as in the "good old days," but the favorite method, next to the railroad trip, is by the

GLEN HOUSE STAGE LINE.

The road is eight miles in length, and by skillful engineering has been so built as to rise, on an average, only about one foot in eight, the steepest place being one foot in six, and that for a short distance only, rendering the ascent easy and comfortable. Passengers by way of Gorham, on the Grand Trunk, reach the summit by this method, and then have the privilege of descending by rail on the other side.

MOUNT WASHINGTON CARRIAGE ROAD.

TUCKERMAN'S RAVINE, an immense seam in the side of Mount Washington, may be explored from the summit, or by following up the stream which takes its rise in this gorge. The chasm is filled to a great depth by the snows of winter, which, in the process of melting, form beautiful arches, sometimes visible till late in the summer.

Returning to the base, we are again at the Fabyan House, from which point we may make excursions in various directions, the excellent livery in connection furnishing carriages and trusty drivers, who will act as guides, and give interesting information to those in their charge.

Before proceeding in our onward journey toward the sea, let us retrace our steps for a visit to the famous FRANCONIA VALLEY.

PROFILE HOUSE AND ECHO LAKE, FRANCONIA NOTCH,
WHITE MOUNTAINS, N. H.

Franconia Notch.

FRANCONIA NOTCH.

From Bethlehem station, as previously mentioned, the Profile & Franconia Notch Railroad extends to this resort, which is one of the most popular in the White Mountain region. Its crowning attraction is the celebrated Profile, so widely known as "THE OLD MAN OF THE MOUNTAIN." This colossal copy of the human face is to be seen on the southern side of Profile Mountain, with bold and high forehead, straight nose, slightly parted mouth, and prominent chin. From forehead to chin, the face measures some eighty feet, and the elevation is some fifteen hundred feet above Profile Lake, which, from its location, is sometimes called "The Old Man's Mirror," and "The Old Man's Washbowl."

OLD MAN OF THE MOUNTAIN.—DISTANT VIEW.

Profile House, an elegant and roomy hotel, with accommodations for five hundred guests, is not the least attractive feature of the neighborhood, its great popularity often filling it to overflowing, even before the railroad made it so easy of access. Messrs. Taft & Greenleaf, the proprietors, are among the most successful hotel managers in all the region.

Mount Lafayette, the highest peak of the Franconian range, has an altitude of 5,259 feet, and the view from the summit is regarded as second only to that from Mount Washington. The ascent is made by bridle path from the Profile House, where horses, guides, etc., are to be found at the service of the tourist. A building at the summit affords shelter from inclement weather, or the severe winds which sometimes prevail at such an elevation.

EAGLE CLIFF.

Eagle Cliff, a huge crag, with precipitous front, towers up to the height of fifteen hundred feet, directly in front of the hotel. A pair of eagles made it their home for some years, until driven away by the curiosity of explorers. A fine view of the Cliff is to be had from Echo Lake, which nestles at its base, and is one of the most charming little bodies of water to be found. The blast of a horn, or the report of a small cannon, fired at intervals to "wake the echoes," reverberates against the sides of the Cliff and the rocky walls which environ the lake, with a succession of sharp and distinct repetitions, growing fainter and fainter, and finally dying away among the far-off cliffs, with an effect as beautiful as it is surprising.

NEAR VIEW OF THE PROFILE.

The Profile House stands at the gateway of the Notch, the approach being from the north. On either side of the gorge, the Franconia range extends in a southerly direction. Lafayette, Lincoln and Liberty on the east, Profile. Kinsman and Pemigewasset on the west, with several lesser peaks and spurs, the valley gradually descending to the south, and widening in the descent, until it expands into the Valley of the Pemigewasset.

FRANCONIA MOUNTAINS, FROM PEMIGEWASSET VALLEY.

Three miles from the Profile House, a path diverges from the road near a small brook, and a walk of half a mile brings to view a succession of picturesque waterfalls, which have received the name of WALKER'S FALLS. A half mile further south is the BASIN, a curious granite reservoir, about forty feet across, and twenty-eight feet deep, in which the waters make a gyratory turn, after the whirlpool order.

Five miles from the Profile House, near the lower gateway of the Notch, is the FLUME HOUSE, so named from its proximity to the rocky ravine, between whose walls the Great Boulder is suspended, as though ready to fall at the slightest provocation. As these pages are being printed, the telegraph brings the news that the ravine has been choked by an avalanche, and the fall of the boulder is reported. When the book is in the hands of its readers, the correctness of the report will have been determined, but at this writing it cannot be verified.

MOUNT LAFAYETTE.

FLUME AND BOULDER.

WEIRS STATION AND STEAMBOAT LANDING, LAKE WINNIPESAUKEE.

The Pool, the Cascades, Georgianna Falls, Mount Pemigewasset, and other objects of interest, are to be visited from the Flume House. A stage route extends from the Profile House to Plymouth, *via* the Pemigewasset, and before the completion of the railroad from Bethlehem, was the principal method of conveyance to this locality.

It is still a favorite with many travelers, being, as above indicated, a direct route to PLYMOUTH, a favorite resort on the Boston, Concord, & Montreal Railroad. Those wishing to reach Boston by this route may connect by stage with the trains at Plymouth, or, returning to Bethlehem, may take the trains of this road, which run *via* Wing Road, Littleton, Warren, Wells River, Plymouth and Lake Winnipesaukee, to Concord, thence by Concord, Lowell & Boston Railroad, to the metropolis of New England. This is a popular route between Boston and the mountains, and is very largely patronized in the summer.

Near Warren, on this line, is MOOSILAUKE, a mountain peak of some celebrity, which from its comparatively isolated position, affords a very fine view from its summit. The town boasts of *fifty miles* of trout streams, and several excellent hotels provide good accommodations for such as desire to "drop the line," or spend a season in recreation.

OWL'S HEAD AND MOOSILAUKE MOUNTAIN.

THE PEMIGEWASSET HOUSE, at Plymouth, is the dining station of the B. C. & M. R. R., and has an almost national reputation for the excellence of its cuisine. It is also a favorite summer resort hotel.

The beautiful Lake Winnipesaukee is reached at Weirs Station and Steamboat Landing. This sheet of water, irregular in its boundaries, studded with hundreds of islands, and bordered by some of the finest scenery in the world, has obtained almost a world-wide fame, being visited by thousands of tourists every season. Weirs Station is on the western shore; and within a few years has become celebrated as the location of a permanent camp-ground, occupied in turns by the Methodists, the Unitarians, and the Grand Army of the Republic. Several hotels and summer boarding houses have been built to accommodate the increasing demands of tourists who wish to tarry by the margin of the lake, and enjoy its lovely scenery, and bathe and fish in its waters, or ride over its surface among its myriad islands. Center Harbor, on its north shore, Wolfboro on the east, and Alton Bay on the south, are all well-known summer resorts, and the ride between these points by steamer constitutes a delightful trip. Two boats of considerable size, the "Lady of the Lake," owned by the Boston, Concord & Montreal Railroad, and the "Mount Washington," the property of the Boston & Maine Railroad, together with several smaller craft, constitute the flotilla; and their frequent trips among the islands and between the principal ports just mentioned afford opportunity to enjoy the attractions of Winnipesaukee, and to realize the significance of its Indian title, which is translated "Smile of the Great Spirit."

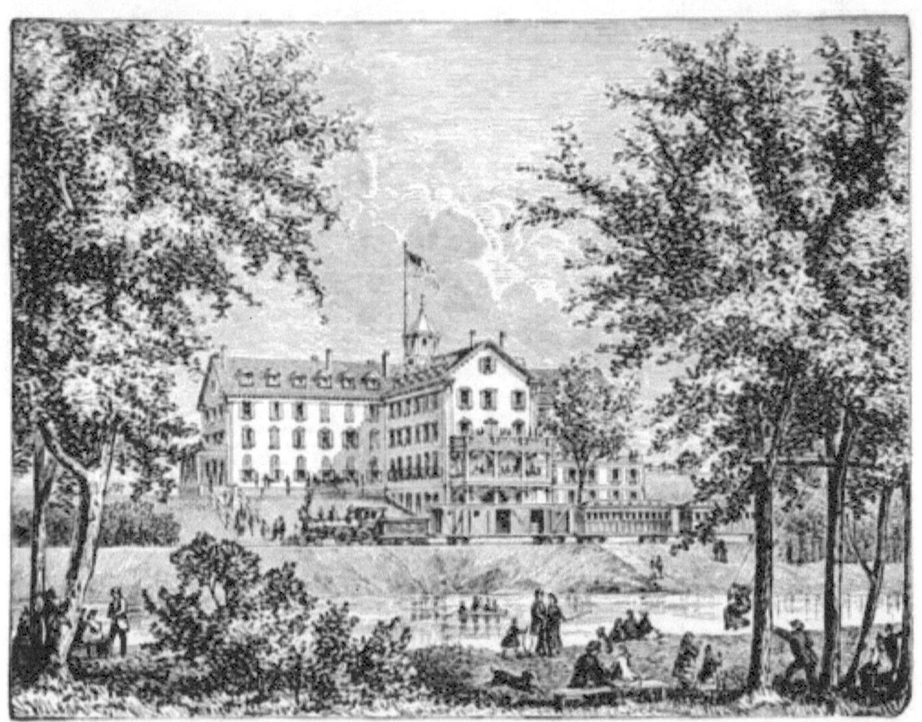

PEMIGEWASSET HOUSE, PLYMOUTH, N. H.

The "Weirs" takes its name from having formerly been the location of the fish-weirs of the aborigines, whence an unlimited supply of food was drawn, in the days before the shriek of the locomotive, or even the crack of the stage-driver's whip, broke the stillness of the adjacent forests.

From Weirs Station the route to Boston is *via* Concord, Manchester, Nashua, and Lowell.

LAKE WINNIPESAUKEE.—STEAMER "LADY OF THE LAKE."

White Mountain Notch.

WHITE MOUNTAIN NOTCH.

The route from Fabyan House to Portland extends through this famous pass, over the Portland & Ogdensburg Railroad; and the ride is one of the most delightful trips by rail to be afforded east of the Rocky Mountains, and with the exception of the ascent to the summit of Mount Washington, is the grandest and most impressive. The railway itself is a wonder, overcoming, in its construction, obstacles that might appall the stoutest-hearted engineer. Running here upon a lofty trestle, clinging now to the side of a mountain, winding around the base of some overhanging cliff, again bridging some mountain stream far above its bed, it threads its devious way through the pass, abolishing the fatigue and hardship incident to mountain visiting, and affording a panoramic view of scenery unsurpassed for variety, novelty and grandeur.

The trip through the Notch is made in Observation Cars, which are attached to all trains. These are open at the sides, and provided with revolving arm chairs, thus affording an outlook in all directions, adding materially to the pleasure of the journey. The first five miles accomplished, and we are at

THE CRAWFORD HOUSE,

Almost in the very gates of the Notch, near its upper entrance. Either in going or returning, this will be found a desirable stopping place, as there are many points of interest in this vicinity. The hotel itself is spacious and elegant, accommodating 500 guests. In the days of mountain-climbing by "brute force," it was the starting point of the bridle path to the summit of Mount Washington; but the hardy mountain ponies, trusty and sure-footed, have given way to the "iron horse," no less trusty, but vastly less romantic.

Saco Lake, near the house, is the source of Saco River, here a diminutive stream, but increasing in volume on its way to the sea, as it absorbs the brooklets and rivulets, until it is utilized in turning the busy wheels of industrious machinery in many a factory before it is lost in the Atlantic.

Gibbs' Falls, also near the hotel, are forty feet in height, divided by a rocky cliff into two parts. They were named in honor of a former landlord of the house.

Beecher's Cascade, a half mile distant, may have had some other name, but it is now lost in the distinction given it by a baptism experienced by the eminent divine, not according to the method of Plymouth Church, but more after the Roger Williams standard, and wholly involuntary.

CRAWFORD HOUSE, WHITE MOUNTAIN NOTCH.

Mount Willard, sometimes called Mount Tom, or Tom Willard, although not of great altitude, furnishes an excellent point of observation from its summit, which is reached by a comfortable carriage ride. The view is highly praised by good judges, Anthony Trollope declaring it unequaled in all the classic Rhineland. Standing at the very gate of the Notch, it commands an excellent view of the chasm, and the different mountains which encompass it, together with a splendid prospect to the west and north.

HERMIT'S POOL, FRANCONIA NOTCH.

SILVER CASCADE and the FLUME CASCADE are two of the attractions of the locality, which leap down the sides of Mount Webster in glorious disorder, now spreading out over a rocky bed in a thin sheet of silver, gathering again in some pool for a plunge over a precipice, breaking into spray in the descent, then running swiftly in a narrow channel as if gathering momentum for another grand leap, and so laughing, singing and dancing on its way, to join the Saco in its noisy pilgrimage to the sea.

THE WILLEY HOUSE, memorable as the scene of the disaster known in history as the "Willey Slide," is located under the steep acclivity of Mount Willey, which rises some 2,000 feet above the house. Opposite are the frowning cliffs of Mount Webster, with the Saco River flowing near. The story of the fearful calamity is familiar, but its repetition may be of interest to our readers. On the night of August 28, 1826, a terrible storm occurred, swelling the brooklets into angry torrents, and loosening the soil from its hold on the rocky acclivity of Mount Willey, sending it down the mountain side with a fearful roar, threatening destruction to everything in its path. Mr. Willey, his wife, five children, and two hired men, comprised the inmates of the house; and it is supposed that they became frightened and fled from the house to escape the peril, and rushed into the very jaws of death, being overwhelmed in the avalanche, not one escaping to tell the tale. The faithful house-dog, however, appeared at Conway, and endeavored to give intelligence of what had happened by all the resources of his power of communication. The bodies of six of the victims were recovered, but three of the children found permanent burial in the *debris*. The saddest feature of the calamity is the fact that had they remained in the house no harm would have befallen them, as a large rock at the back of the house divided the slide, and sent it by on either side, leaving the building untouched. The scarred side of the mountain still shows the track of the avalanche, only enough soil being left to support a growth of white birches.

AVALANCHE BROOK, so called from being regarded as the cause of the disaster, has on it a beautiful cataract, called the SYLVAN GLADE CATARACT, and higher up, another called SPARKLING CASCADE.

Such of the forgoing objects of interest as are visible from the train are pointed out by the conductor and trainmen, and an occasional halt is made to permit of a longer view of some point of special importance. If time will permit, it is well to stop off at one or more of the stations, and proceed by following trains. But whether this be your privilege or not, the ride will be one not soon forgotten, and its repetition desired and longed for.

Below Willey Mountain the valley opens out into a wider expanse, and the scenery becomes less wild and romantic, but none the less beautiful with the change. The Willey-Brook Bridge is a fine specimen of engineering skill, and is crossed by the train, giving the courageous passengers a chance to peer into the deep gulf which it spans, and the timid ones occasion to "hold their breath" at the thought of a possible tumble, should "anything happen." The bridge, however, gives no occasion for fear, as it is of enormous strength, although not ponderous in appearance.

SCENES IN THE WHITE MOUNTAIN NOTCH.—P. & O. RAILROAD.

A short distance below this point, the train crosses the famous FRANKENSTEIN TRESTLE, an iron structure five hundred feet long and eighty feet high. Near this are the GIANT'S STAIRS, MOUNT RESOLUTION and MOUNT CRAWFORD, the latter nearly opposite Bemis Station. Near here is the old Mount Crawford House, now closed, where Abel Crawford, the pioneer for whom the Mountain and Notch were named, "kept tavern" for many years, and told stories and legends of the mountains to his guests, and, on occasion, piloted them to the haunts of the shy trout, or to mountain summits, by paths long forgotten. His son, Ethan Allen Crawford, cut the first bridle path to Mount Washington, in 1821.

VALLEY OF THE SACO RIVER.

Nancy's Brook is soon reached and crossed, so named from a sad incident involving the old story of a deserted maiden, and a recreant lover who fled on the eve of the appointed wedding day, pursued by the poor girl, who perished from exposure, and was found in the snow at the foot of a tree, near the margin of the stream which now bears the name her mother gave her, a kindly way of commemorating the event without involving the family name.

Sawyer's River is crossed, as the road turns sharply to the eastward, and at Upper Bartlett the interesting landmark known as Sawyer's Rock commemorates the discovery of this pass, or rather the accomplishment of an event which attested its discovery, viz., getting a horse through the Notch, for which feat, as an evidence of the existence of the pass, Nash, the discoverer, and a brother hunter, received from Governor Wentworth a grant of land known as Nash & Sawyer's Location. The last obstacle being this rock, the poor beast was let down over it by means of ropes, and Sawyer exultingly dashed his rum bottle against it, which sufficed to christen it by the name it now bears.

At GLEN STATION, connection is made with the stage line for the Glen House up the valley of Ellis River and through Pinkham Notch. Should the traveler feel disposed to make this trip, he will find much to reward him in the way of picturesque scenery, pleasant drives, etc. At a short distance from the road where it crosses Ellis River, a fine waterfall, known as GOODRICH FALLS may be seen. Passing the little village of "Jackson City," the road soon enters the pass known as PINKHAM NOTCH, named from a family of early settlers, who constructed the Notch road.

GLEN-ELLIS FALL.

GLEN-ELLIS FALL may be reached by a path diverging from the stage road. The Ellis River here descends a precipice seventy feet high. From its configuration it was formerly called "Pitcher Fall," but the more poetic but less descriptive title seems to cling to it.

THE GLEN HOUSE,

Previously mentioned as a fine hostelry, is the terminus of the stage line. Here you will meet guests who have come by stage from Gorham, eight miles distant, on the Grand Trunk Railway, or from the summit of Mount Washington, by the carriage road already described. This location is more than sixteen hundred feet above sea-level, and the clear, bracing atmosphere, the magnificent scenery, and the delightful drives in several directions, together with the excellent manner in which the hotel is kept, are sufficient to account for its popularity and success. In the matter of stage-line management, it probably has no superior in the world, that which conveys the passengers up the carriage road to the summit of Mount Washington being notably superior in point of equipment, and the well-known skill of its drivers.

Excursions may be made from here to the Carter Notch, Osgood's Cascades, Summit of Mount Madison, Garnet Pools, Emerald Pool, Thompson's Falls, Glen-Ellis Falls, Crystal Cascade, Tuckerman's Ravine, and many other places of more than ordinary interest.

APPROACH TO NORTH CONWAY.—P. & O. R. R.

But again taking up our line of travel at Glen Station, the train soon emerges upon the beautiful Conway Intervales, Intervale Station being the next stopping place. The Intervale House, near by, is a pleasant abode for those who choose to tarry. A short distance beyond is North Conway, a village of multitudinous attractions, and with a popularity as a summer resort that is surprising to the casual visitor, who, although seeing much to admire, fails to comprehend the peculiar combinations which bring people year after year to spend their summers in the vicinity. Superficially, the most attractive objects conspicuously visible are the hotels. The spacious Kiarsarge House seems a veritable paradise for the traveler, and its tables are unexcelled. The views from its verandahs are superior, comprising the mountain ranges, the famous Pequaket or Kiarsarge Mountain, and the lovely Intervales, upon which the village is situated. The mountain from which the hotel receives its name is about three miles from the village, and the ascent may be made in the saddle or on foot. The altitude is 3,367 feet, and the view from the summit comprises the entire White Mountain Range, together with Mote Mountain, Rattlesnake Ridge, Sebago Lake with other bodies of water of less magnitude, and a stretch of landscape in every direction most pleasing to the eye, less grand and rugged, to be sure, than that we have been describing, but on that account more restful to the senses.

KIARSARGE HOUSE AND MOUNTAIN.—DISTANT VIEW.

The other attractions at North Conway consist of Artist's Falls, Echo Lake, the Cathedral and Ledges, Diana's Baths, the Devil's Den, and a host of lovely drives in various directions, with sylvan paths for pedestrianism *ad libitum*.

Conway Center, five miles southeast of North Conway, is the next station, and has many charms as a summer resort. Mount Chocorua, with a sharp pinnacle, towering up 3,540 feet above sea-level, is reached from here to good advantage, as is also Walker Pond, a short distance south of the town.

We are now in the "smiling valley" of the Saco River, in the midst of cultivated farms and peaceful villages, in striking contrast with the scenery just left behind. Crossing the boundary line between New Hampshire and Maine, our next station is Fryeburg, which some poetic writer has called the "Queen of the Saco Valley." It is indeed a lovely town, embowered in deep foliage, and affording the visitor most delightful drives. Jockey Cap, a huge granite pile, is near the village; and close by is Lovewell's Pond, the scene of an Indian battle in 1725. Mount Pleasant is only seven miles distant, and has upon its summit a fine hotel.

MOUNT KIARSARGE, OR PEQUAKET.

Passing in quick succession the stations of Brownfield, Hiram, the three Bald-wins, and Steep Falls, we reach

SEBAGO LAKE,

Seventeen miles from Portland, and forty-three from North Conway. For a short distance before reaching the lake, the run is devoid of interest and exceedingly tame; but as the road skirts the shores of this beautiful sheet of water, and its broad expanse stretches away in the distance, bounded by wooded shores and sandy beaches, the change is magical, and the contrast a most pleasing one. Sebago itself is twelve miles long and nine miles wide, and is connected with Long Pond by means of Songo River and the "Bay of Naples," formerly "Brandy Pond," —before the days of the "Maine law." The entire chain of lakes, river and bay affords a steamboat ride of sixty-eight miles in the round trip. Bridgton, one of the steam-er-landings on Long Pond, is the birth-place of the genial humorist "Artemus Ward." From Portland, a pleasant and popular trip consists of a ride to Sebago by the morning train, a trip over the lake to Bridgton, returning in time for the evening train to Portland.

CITY AND HARBOR OF PORTLAND, FROM CAPE ELIZABETH.

And thither, in the continuation of our excursion, we too must go. Only seventeen miles more of our long and delightful journey "from Chicago to the Sea" remain to be traversed. Almost regretfully we linger over the few last leagues of the trip, but remembering that either way from Portland our excursion may be lengthened indefinitely, we resume our seats in the train, and in fifty minutes are in

THE METROPOLIS OF MAINE.

PORTLAND is pleasantly situated on a narrow peninsula projecting from the west shore of Casco Bay. This peninsula is about three miles in length from east to west, with considerable elevations at each end, giving the city a beautiful appearance as approached from the sea. Its harbor is one of the best on the Atlantic coast, being deep and capacious, and protected by land on all sides. The city is beautifully laid out, its public buildings are fine, and many of its private residences elegant.

The commercial and business interests of the city are extensive and important, the value of the shipping owned in the district being very great, and its manufactures employing a large amount of capital. The railroads centering here are the Portland & Ogdensburg, Portland & Rochester, Boston & Maine, Eastern, Maine Central, and Grand Trunk.

The leading hotels of Portland are the Falmouth, United States, Preble, City, Kirkland, and Merchants.

The climate of Portland is remarkably salubrious, the city being peculiarly exempt from epidemics, or climatic diseases of any kind. The source of water supply (Sebago Lake), and the excellent facilities for drainage, undoubtedly contribute much to the healthfulness of the locality. These circumstances, together with the proximity of beaches and other resorts, render Portland a desirable place for summer sojourning, a fact of which no little advantage is taken in the season of travel. The steamship lines running from Portland to eastern ports along the coast of Maine and the maritime provinces, afford the tourist opportunities to extend his trip "away down East," as far as time and inclination will permit. One resort of special interest deserves mention while this subject is under consideration, on account of its remarkable attractiveness, and its increasing popularity.

MOUNT DESERT ISLAND,

One hundred and ten miles northeast from Portland, is reached by the PORTLAND, BANGOR AND MACHIAS STEAMBOAT LINE, whose boats make connection with the trains from Boston and the White Mountains. They are staunch and seaworthy, and finely equipped; and the trip along the shore, past the thrifty villages, and among the picturesque scenery, is full of delights.

The island of Mount Desert lies quite near the mainland, with which communication is had by means of a bridge which crosses at Trenton. In shape, the island is quite irregular, and is about eighteen miles long by twelve wide. It is nearly divided in two by Somes Sound, and its shores on all sides are indented by picturesque bays and inlets. The greater part of its surface is covered with mountain peaks, some thirteen in number, the highest, Mt. Green, rising fully two thousand feet above the sea. High up among these peaks are several beautiful lakes, which, with the streams that flow from them, abound in trout.

BAR HARBOR, MOUNT DESERT ISLAND.

The first landing point, approaching from Portland, is SOUTHWEST HARBOR. Here are several excellent hotels, and the scenery in the vicinity, and accessible by pleasant carriage drives, is beautiful and picturesque. Green Mountain is reached from this point to good advantage by the westerly slope, a carriage road leading to the summit, where a hotel is located.

BAR HARBOR, fifteen miles beyond Southwest Harbor, is even more picturesque and romantic in its location than the latter. The scenery along the coast is bold and impressive, stupendous cliffs rising abruptly to the height of several hundred feet. Bar Harbor is plentifully supplied with hotels, and their facilities are often utilized by the throngs of artists and pleasure-seekers who make summer pilgrimages in search of the beautiful, the art galleries and studios of the country testifying to the success of the former in transferring to canvas the gems of scenery which have formed the basis of so many studies and afforded so much delight.

In addition to the many "down-east" trips that may be made from Portland, its nearness to some of the fine beaches of the Atlantic coast is another of its attractions as an objective point for the tourist. Two great railway lines connect Portland with Boston, and one or both of them reach all the principal intervening seaside resorts.

One of the most noted of these is

OLD ORCHARD BEACH.

This celebrated seaside camp-ground,—for as a place for temperance and religious camp-meetings it is best known,—is reached by the BOSTON & MAINE RAILROAD, extensively advertised by its managers as the "shore route" between Boston and Portland. And it may not be amiss to say, in this connection, that it is really one of the finest equipped and best managed railroads in the country. Its general superintendent, Mr. J. T. Furber, is one of the successful railroad managers of New England, a tireless worker, looking after every detail of the road and its operation, with a degree of energy and "push" that marks the successful business man wherever you meet him in Yankeedom.

Old Orchard not only has a vast expanse of beautiful beach, but possesses the additional charm of woodland parks and groves, hundreds of acres in extent, stretching away from the shore, enclosing cool retreats and shady paths, where the forest has been left almost in its primeval state. This happy combination of "woods and seashore" in one locality, affording a pleasing variety and gratifying the tastes of all, is one secret of the great popularity of this resort. The splendid hotel, so conspicuous in the background of our illustration, is kept in a style to please the most fastidious, it being the leading hotel of this vicinity. The less pretentious house in the foreground is a great favorite with many visitors, not only for its home-like air, but for the beautiful views to be had from its verandahs and the charming walks and drives in the vicinity. Its patrons speak of it in terms of the highest commendation.

WELLS BEACH and KENNEBUNKPORT are also reached by the Boston & Maine Railroad, and are among the long list of popular resorts on the eastern coast. The latter has an elegant hotel, the "Ocean Bluff," which commands a beautiful view of ocean and landscape combined.

OLD ORCHARD BEACH.

At Dover, on the main line to Boston, connection is made with the Winnipesaukee division to ALTON BAY, a celebrated summer and camp-ground resort, at the head of the bay, which is an arm of the beautiful Lake Winnipesaukee, extending in a southerly direction. The steamer MOUNT WASHINGTON makes frequent trips from this point to Wolfboro and Center Harbor, from either of which places connection is made for the Weirs, on the Boston, Concord & Montreal Railroad, by steamer "Lady of the Lake."

The EASTERN RAILROAD, the other through line between Portland and Boston, reaches several of the beaches already mentioned, and is the direct route to HAMPTON and RYE BEACHES, BOAR'S HEAD, and and REVERE BEACH, the latter sustaining the same relation to Boston as does Coney Island to New York.

THE ISLES OF SHOALS, nine miles off Portsmouth harbor, are also reached by the Eastern Railroad to Portsmouth, thence by steamer to Appledore and Star Islands, where two palace hotels, the APPLEDORE, on the island of the same name, and the OCEANIC on Star Island, are kept in regal style by Laighton Brothers & Co. The group comprises nine islands, the largest of which is Appledore. It is also the best known, having been for many years the favorite summer home of many of the prominent literary people of New England. It is the residence of Mrs. Celia (Laighton) Thaxter, whose pleasing poems have gratified so many readers; and her childhood was spent in this lovely spot, the very air of which is full of poetic inspiration.

White Island is the location of a light-house which the readers of the *Atlantic Monthly* will remember as the scene of many of the pleasing incidents in Mrs. Thaxter's "Child Life at the Isles of Shoals."

IN RETURNING FROM THE SEA,

The excursionist may traverse again the route through the mountains, — and some portions of it are well worthy of a second visit, or by a different route may reach the St. Lawrence River, and find new objects and scenes to claim his attention. Should the latter be his choice, he may take the train of the Concord & Portsmouth Railroad, at Portsmouth, and go *via* Manchester, Concord, White River Junction and St. Albans to Ogdensburg or Montreal, thence homeward by the St. Lawrence River, or the rail route, as preferred.

Many, however, will wish to see Boston or New York; and a pleasant trip, comprising a visit to these two cities, may be made by boat or rail from Portland to Boston, thence by Long Island Sound to New York. The Sound Steamer Lines are four in number, all of them having an initial stage by rail to some point on the Sound where connection is made with the boats.

THE FALL RIVER LINE comprises a trip by rail from Boston to Fall River, forty-nine miles, there transferring to one of the floating palaces, the "Bristol," the "Providence," or the new and elegant "Pilgrim," the latter being conceded to be the finest boat on the Sound. J. R. Kendrick, Esq., is the general manager of this line, with headquarters at Boston, and Geo. L. Connor is the general passenger agent, located in New York.

THE STONINGTON LINE has for its inception the rail route to Stonington, Connecticut, *via* Providence, where connection is made with the elegant steamers, "Massachusetts" and "Rhode Island." This route has more of rail and less of water than the preceding, and avoids the "outside" passage around Point Judith, a consideration that has its weight with the timid and sensitive.

THE PROVIDENCE LINE is under the same management as that of the foregoing, and comprises a rail trip to Providence, and boat from there to New York, the steamers "Stonington" and "Narragansett" being employed on this line.

THE NORWICH LINE has for its beginning a rail trip to New London, thence by steamer to New York.

The start from Boston is in the early evening, the arrival at the various boat landings being in ample season for "bed-time," and the trip through the Sound is a night ride, arriving in New York in season to connect with morning trains if desired. The passengers who arise in moderately good season will enjoy the latter portion of the ride, as the boat enters the famous passage known as "Hell Gate," passes down the East River in view of the islands on which are located the various reformatory, penal, and charitable institutions of New York City, continuing between the cities of New York and Brooklyn, under the famous suspension bridge, and around the Battery and Castle Garden into the North River. The shipping in the harbor, the sprightly tugs steaming here and there, the ferry boats plying between Long Island and New York, and the ceaseless activity and bustle of all things animate, all combine to give to the scene an air of life and vigor so characteristic of all that pertains to the great metropolis of America.

The sights and scenes of the city itself are so numerous and varied that the pen falters at the thought of even attempting to mention them. If the reader has a desire to "do" the city in a systematic and thorough manner, he should secure the company of some one familiar with its customs and its places of interest, or consult the pages of some city guide book.

FROM NEW YORK TO THE WEST.

The return to the West from New York City may be made by several different routes, at the option of the tourist. THE NEW YORK CENTRAL AND HUDSON RIVER RAILROAD affords a pleasant ride up the Hudson River, among its beautiful scenery to Albany, thence across the State to Suspension Bridge or Buffalo. The new WEST SHORE line, by a nearly parallel route, traverses the other side of the Hudson, and will soon be completed for through travel. The trip up the Hudson by boat is also a favorite in the summer season, as affording the finest views of the points of interest that have given to this river the title of the "Rhine of America."

For picturesque scenery, no route can be regarded as equal to the NEW YORK, LAKE ERIE AND WESTERN, familiarly known as the "Erie Line." Crossing the ferry to Jersey City, the passenger by this line finds the trains of this road awaiting at the station, with through cars attached for Buffalo, Rochester, and the principal Western points. Leaving Jersey City by the morning train, the tourist will find that the day's ride among the picturesque mountain, river, and lake scenery all along the line will be one of great interest and enjoyment. The courtesy and urbanity of the trainmen and conductors are especially noticeable, and the eating houses, at which ample time is given for meals, are among the best railroad restaurants it is the privilege of the traveler to visit.

Connection is made at Buffalo with the Canada Southern division of the Michigan Central, from which point the return may be made *via* Detroit, to the starting point of the journey.

BOSTON TO THE WEST.

The return trip from Boston, omitting the visit to New York, may be made very direct, should the tourist so elect. The short line from Boston, and on many accounts a very pleasant one, is *via* the celebrated HOOSAC TUNNEL, comprising the Fitchburg Railroad to North Adams, and the Troy & Boston Railroad to Troy, thence *via* the New York Central to Suspension Bridge or Buffalo. This route presents the advantages of through sleeping coaches from Boston to Chicago, without change, a most desirable feature for families or for ladies traveling alone.

The line takes its name from the wonderful tunnel through Hoosac Mountain, which opens a roadway for the locomotive directly across the State of Massachusetts. This immense engineering enterprise was begun in 1862, on the supposition that the internal structure of the mountain would be found of a character to admit of easy excavation. The undertaking proved, however, that its projectors had been misled by the geologists, and solid rock was the substance to be removed for the greater part of nearly five miles. At an immense cost, the excavation was carried on, and in 1875 was open for the passage of trains, and later was perfected by arches of masonry where strengthening was necessary.

The equipment of the "Tunnel Line" is complete and in all respects first class. The starting point in Boston is from the depot of the Fitchburg Railroad, of which John Adams, Esq., is the genial and popular superintendent. The Western office of the line is in Chicago, at 135 Randolph Street, in charge of C. E. Lambert, Esq., the general Western passenger agent.

The return from Boston may also be made by way of Springfield and Albany, by the Boston & Albany Railroad, thence by the New York Central to Buffalo or Suspension Bridge.

And now, having taken the reader, in imagination, from his home in the West to the Atlantic seaboard, through some of the most delightful scenery on the American Continent, and indicated a variety of routes by which he may return, with a few closing words the duty of the writer will be done. Possibly no one traveler or party will traverse all the routes described in this work. In some cases we have indicated that choice may be made of several methods of reaching a given point, and the taste or preference of the tourist, or the convenience of a party traveling in company, will often decide the route. We have endeavored to give fair and impartial description of the attractions offered by the various lines of travel,—often too painfully conscious of the inadequacy of words to do justice to the subject considered,—and leave the reader to choose for himself a route from among the variety set forth.

Before closing, we will add that a large variety of excursion tickets will be found on sale at the principal ticket offices of the Michigan Central Railroad, from which a selection can be made in accordance with your taste or preferences. If the perusal of this work has assisted in deciding your route, you will probably be able to secure a ticket through to the sea to accommodate your wishes. By a very convenient arrangement, your choice of a portion of the route may be left until arriving at the St. Lawrence River, when the purser of the steamer will exchange your ticket, giving opportunity to select from a variety of excursions, with added side trips to various points of interest.

And now, with a consciousness of its many imperfections, we bring this work to a close, and take a regretful leave of the reader, with the hope that the pages of the book may prove serviceable in making enjoyable the journey of many a tourist

From Chicago to the Sea.

INDEX.

Lector House believes that a society develops through a two-fold approach of continuous learning and adaptation, which is derived from the study of classic literary works spread across the historic timeline of literature records. Therefore, we aim at reviving, repairing and redeveloping all those inaccessible or damaged but historically as well as culturally important literature across subjects so that the future generations may have an opportunity to study and learn from past works to embark upon a journey of creating a better future.

This book is a result of an effort made by Lector House towards making a contribution to the preservation and repair of original ancient works which might hold historical significance to the approach of continuous learning across subjects.

HAPPY READING & LEARNING!

LECTOR HOUSE LLP
E-MAIL: lectorpublishing@gmail.com